Theology in
Winter Light

Enda McDonagh

the columba press

First edition, 2010, published by
the columba press
55A Spruce Avenue, Stillorgan Industrial Park,
Blackrock, Co Dublin

Cover by Bill Bolger
Origination by The Columba Press
Printed in Ireland by
Colour Books Ltd, Dublin

ISBN 978 1 85607 683-8

Acknowledgements

The author and publisher acknowledge the permission of Faber and Faber Ltd to quote *Postscript* by Seamus Heaney, and of Bloodaxe Books for permission to quote *The Bright Field* by R. S. Thomas.

As ever, I am greatly indebted for the help of my secretetary, Mary O Malley, for the helpful advice and co-operation of Ronan Drury, Editor of *The Furrow* and his secretary, Maria Flood, for the innumerable advice and provocation of theological and other friends and, of course, Seán O Boyle and his staff at The Columba Press.

The editors of the publications which some of these pieces already appeared (now in more or less revised form) I also wish to thank. These publications are listed herewith: Ch 2, *The Furrow*, June 2009; Ch 3, *Contemporary Irish Moral Discourse*, Ed Amelia Fleming, Dublin 2007; Ch 4, *Remembering to Forgive*, Ed Enda Mc Donagh, Dublin 2008; Ch 6, *The Furrow*, March 2009; Ch 7, *The Furrow*, October 2008; Ch 8, *Moral Theology for the Twenty-First Century*, Eds Clague, Hoose, Mannion, London 2008; Ch 9, *The Furrow*, January 2009; Ch 10, *Studies*, Autumn 2008; Ch 11, *Irish Theological Quarterly*, Summer 2008; Ch 12, *Dublin Review of Books*, Spring 2009; Ch 13, *Unquiet Spirit*, Ed Yseult Thornley, Dublin 2009; Ch 14, *The Furrow*, May 2007; Ch 15 *What Being a Catholic Means to Me*, Eds Littleton and Maher, Dublin 2009; Ch 16, *Doctrine and Life*, January 2009.

Contents

A Tribute to the Students and Staff at St Patrick's College, Maynooth, 1948-2010'

INTRODUCTION

From Summer Dazzle to Winter Light

Given the weather in Mayo, where I am struggling to write, the shift can happen in a matter of hours. (Oh for Longley's 'Weather In Japan'!) The timescale for theology is somewhat longer, in the case of this theologian almost sixty years from First Theology beyond formal retirement to successive postscripts. And that fails to take account of the almost three thousand years of living biblical and Christian witness which provide essential background and resources to any Christian theologian. Let's settle, however, just now for the sixty years foreground as the immediate field of play of this particular volume. This is not to preclude the continuing and direct influence of the previous three thousand years or to suggest that the material in this volume ranges over all the writings of the last sixty years. In fact these writings are confined to the last three years and offer only a selection from these years. Of course they pick up themes from what the theologian might be tempted to regard not only as his summer-time but the summer-time and summer dazzle of the modern church in the years of Vatican II. These themes must be reconsidered in the light of what Karl Rahner already some thirty years ago or so called the 'Winter-time of the church' and which, in the present writer's view, has become a much more wintry time. That view may be influenced unduly by his own deeper entry into 'winter light' and his nostalgic return to some old themes and old dreams. Happily new dreams do occur and can provoke a second, third or fourth spring, if not quite summer dazzle.

In winter light the theologian's vision may well be sharpened, as the luxuriant growth of earlier reading and youthful concerns drop away and s/he is forced to focus on the more persistent, permanent and oft-times perturbing. Not that the perturbances are necessarily depressing, they may also be exciting and even uplifting as some settled and oppressive order in church or state is seriously shaken. In this winter and its light such perturbances are readily evident and in many senses truly welcome. Whether the shaking will lead to much needed reform of structures and personnel in banks, government or church chanceries and their practices remains as yet opaque. The winter light exposes the reach of the destruction without discerning the shape of reform. It does prompt the obvious question: 'Can the destroyers also be the reformers?'

The essays collected here are not finally focused on the boom to bust cycle which has afflicted the Irish economy, the Irish political system and the Irish church, although these series of events are an inevitable influence. The world of the theologian is wider and one hopes deeper than such happenings, important as they are, above all for the people nearer the bottom of the pile than for the architects of our misfortunes. Indeed these wider and deeper concerns may help a little by shedding their winter light on the causes of the destruction and by motivating and encouraging the necessary reconstruction. At least this is the fragile hope of the author as he marshals his recent efforts to make sense of Christian life and love in what seems increasingly a situation of exile from, and yet belonging to, a more alien church and society.

In ecclesial, cultural, social, political and economic life there is at present much to lament but also much to celebrate when one refuses to be trapped by the imperial 'Now' of media preoccupations. That imperial 'Now' of course moves with the next day's or week's or month's headlines, and the headlines display a morbid obsession with the disastrous. In almost eighty years of listening to or reading the headlines from local gossip to political, economic and church lectures, to national and international media, one still has to be alert for the good news behind the bad, for the 'so much' we have to be grateful for and the 'so much' we have to be hopeful for. Real gratitude and real hope, however, have to be rooted in recognition of the genuine bad news in which the good is always embedded. Winter light, given the experience including the past mistakes of the observer, may help sharpen discernment of the good from the bad. Or it may not. Memory grows more faulty while detachment from old hurts and prejudices may even decline. Despite these inevitable limitations, winter light can bring fresh truth and consolation.

As a theologian my professional focus has been on Christianity as a way of life founded in the truth and love manifest in Jesus Christ. This involves both vision and virtue – theory and practice as some contemporaries might put it. Many aspects of both vision and virtue are as old as the earliest Hebrew scriptures, some are as new as the latest developments in war or medicine. In the long meantime, variations occur and recur in the continuing history of humankind in action and reflection. Some of this continuity and discontinuity is experienced by every human individual and society. The rather crude divisions of this collection attempt to mirror this experience, not in any chronological sequence but in the related mental preoccupations of recent winter years.

Part I, *Old Themes,* reviews some earlier concerns in moral exploration of Christian living. One of my first major investigations dealt with the relations between church and state in Catholic theology in the 1950s and 1960s prior to, and subsequent to, the two influential documents of Vatican II, the *Pastoral Constitition on the Church in the Modern World* and the *Declaration on Religious Freedom.* I doubt if a year has passed since in which I have not commented on these issues in lecture, article or book. Naturally the focus has shifted over the years. My most recent comment was presented at a Conference in Castlebar (April, 2009) on a New Vision for Ireland, as an effort to respond to the financial and political collapse of the previous months. While others more competent dealt directly with some of the financial, political and social issues, I addressed Irish failures in public morality as failures in moral imagination under the title, *Public and Corporate Ethics.* I developed this a little further in a piece dedicated to Seamus Heaney for his seventieth birthday, *'Inwardness' and the Economic Crisis.*

More regular Christian moral themes emerged in the following chapters on justice, marriage and forgiveness, although they record, I hope, some advance in my own thinking. Finally, I return courtesy of Professor Patrick Masterson's fine book to one of the major themes of all religious moral analysts – to the relation be-

tween reason and God – with a concluding reflection on the very
Word of God, source of all Christian writing.

Part II is rather boldly entitled *New Dreams*. The distinctions are
not entirely clear-cut as new and old merge in and out of one another. Yet there is sufficient newness in subject matter and treatment to justify the distinction. The most obvious overlap and yet
the sharpest contrast of new and old occurs in *The Good News of
Moral Theology* in honour of that outstanding moral theologian in
Britain, Kevin Kelly. Its subtitle, 'Of Hospitality, Healing and
Hope' as characteristic of Christian moral thinking and activity,
gives a hint of the newness. *The Kenosis of Preaching* emphasises the
cost to the preacher of preaching the good news as a way of life.
The following three chapters engage with Irish artists and Irish art
in seeking to go beneath the prosaic thinking of much theology
and ethics, in responding to the poetry of Thomas Kinsella and
John F Deane and the beautiful sculpture work of Imogen Stuart.
In *The Catholic Intellectual*, a memorial piece on the occasion of the
thirtieth anniversary of the premature death of academic, politi-
cian, TV presenter and friend, David Thornley, attends to the much
neglected role of the intellectual in church and society in Ireland.

Part III, *In Winter Light*, sets a more sombre tone. *A communion of
sinners* takes a more realistic look at the church in its present crises.
The Burying Priest concentrates on the centrality to the older priest
of the death of parishioners, family and friends and the spiritual
cost of all that. *...should vatican two fail ...* is a typical winter light
fear especially in the sad aftermath of the death of one of its great
Irish advocates, editor and social activist, Austin Flannery OP.

Almost all these essays have been written in response to particular invitations and most of them in response to friends living
and dead. Increasingly this is how I tend to work, partly from
pressures of time and partly from love of people and causes. They
have been selected from a rather larger range of essays published
in the 2007-2009 period as making a more coherent unit.

PART ONE: OLD THEMES

CHAPTER ONE

Public and Corporate Ethics

Economics has long been the new politics and Ireland Inc has long been the dominant symbol of successful Irish politics. With the sharp and rapid decline of its ambitious and even arrogant claims of unlimited growth, economics, or more likely just money, may become the new sex, with its daily tawdry revelations filling our newssheets, airwaves and screens to the shock horror-delight of reporters and their audiences. Then come the self-righteous denunciations of many who were happy to enjoy the dubious rewards of such unethical political, banking and other financial and economic practices, as long as they did not know of them officially or could assert as much . Of course that list of 'unknowing' beneficiaries were never among the poorest or more deserving in the land, although one must now attend to their very real losses and needs. Yet after the most stringent 'corrective measures', the really poor and deprived will as usual suffer disproportionately. Sharing the pain fairly now may prove as difficult as getting the wealthy tax evaders and exiles to share the tax burden fairly in the past and present.

As the revelations and denunciations are more than adequately treated in the regular media I may be forgiven here for simply taking their reality for granted without having to engage in much finger pointing or moral judgement. However in this country at this time it would be impossible to pass over the seeming imbalance in the administration of justice by which such fraudulent and destructive practices are apparently rewarded or at least wriggled out of, while minor and perhaps justified protests such as those of Maura Harrington and the Rossport Five end up in jail. In that lawless country, as it is sometimes portrayed over here, the USA, the Madoffs, the Conrad Blacks and the heads of the Enron Corporation haven't fared so well. One other preliminary point is worth mentioning without further development. The current fiscal, economic and social crisis in its Irish mode is not to be blamed primarily on the lack of education, scientific or technical, but more on the lack of that education in the humanities, including ethics, which good Universities and Institutes can and do provide. My own modest contribution to this Institute's Library is intended to encourage and facilitate the further development of these humane studies.[1]

The Visionary theme of this symposium embraces the more restricted topic allocated to me, 'Reflections on Irish Corporate and Public Ethics'. That requires from me at least some reflection on both vision and ethics and their inter-relation. Indeed the books which I have had the privilege of donating here would, if able to speak through their readers, expect to hear something of the relation between vision and ethics, with which so many of them deal in different ways.

Vision and Ethics: The Poetry and the Prose of Moral Reflection
As there is no absolutely consistently distinctive use of such terms as ethics and morality, I am going to use the term 'morality' as applying immediately and mainly to personal and community activity, in evaluating that activity as right or wrong, good or evil, and in theological discourse as virtuous or sinful. Ethics then arises in reflecting on such activity and its evaluation in what is sometimes rather pompously described as second order moral discourse. All of the above is of secondary importance anyway except to the professionally academic as the rest of this paper may show. Of primary importance here, however, is the less usual distinction between the poetry and prose of moral activity and of reflection on it. This is close to but not identical with the imaginative and the rational approaches to morality and ethics. Within the Western religious and philosophical traditions of morality these two approaches have been at work in ways not always recognised. The poetic and imaginative has its origins in the Hebrew prophets and in the preaching and teaching of Jesus Christ in the New

---

1. This lecture was given on the occasion of the official opening by Mary Robinson of the library which I had presented to GMIT, Castlebar, on 4 April 2009.

Testament; imaginative and poetic examples could be found in the Sermon on Mount, many of the parables and the summation of the whole Law and the Prophets in Love of God and Love of Neighbour. The prosal (to avoid using 'prosaic') and rational dominate in Greeks such as Aristotle and, with a more severely rational character, in the work of Immanuel Kant and his European and Anglo-Saxon successors. The most significant attempt at synthesis between the two traditions was that of Thomas Aquinas in the thirteenth century with his primacy of charity as the form of all the virtues, virtues whose structure and meaning were mainly derived from Aristotle and consolidated in the complex called Natural Law. Since then there has been both more divergence between and confusion of the formative roles of the imaginative and the rational in morality and ethics, with a culture-bound and narrow scientific calculating version of the rational prevailing. However, in other admittedly imaginative areas poetry and prose seem to come naturally and beautifully to such writers as John F Deane , a contributor to this symposium, and Nobel Laureate Seamus Heaney. And there is no reason why lesser mortals like ourselves should not combine our imagination and reason, the poetry and prose of our own lives, in developing the morality and ethics of these lives. I should also mention in this context that the worlds of poetry and banking / finance have seen some powerful and unified personal embodiments in our lifetimes, T. S. Eliot and Wallace Stevens, two of the greatest American poets of the twentieth century, were, respectively, a banker and an executive of a massive Insurance Corporation. Nearer our time and place, living Irish poets Thomas Kinsella and Dennis O Driscoll have worked in the Irish Department of Finance. Kinsella was personal private secretary to T. K. Whittaker when the first plan for Irish economic development was being formulated in 1958. O'Driscoll works in the even more unlikely place, it might seem for a poet, the offices of the Internal Revenue.

I have laboured this introduction as background to some deeper understanding of our present failures in corporate and public ethics and as basis for identifying some resources that might help to overcome them. In search of such understanding and resources we need to examine corporate and public ethics at the different levels at which they operate. In the corporate as in the public world the different participants enjoy diverse organisational roles and responsibilities which may be governed by diverse concepts of right and wrong, and sometimes formulated into particular codes of behaviour. At the immediate level of responsibility, these codes of business ethics, for example, apply to both partners in business dealing to ensure honesty and openness and to protect against fraud by either party. However, the code and its uses frequently derive from and depend on the interests of the more powerful party such as a major corporation in dealing with lesser bodies or individuals, leading at times to exploitation of these lesser bodies and individuals. So shareholders, suppliers and customers may be readily cheated to that double but irreconcilable protest of innocence from some CEO or other official in face of exposure, 'I take full responsibility; I did nothing wrong.' And we have had our fair share of such protests in the recent crisis.

Above and beyond the self-regulation of corporate behaviour is the civil law, the attempt by society to strengthen the regulation of corporations and protect the public and their clients from their depredations. Light-touch regulation, encouraged in some cases no doubt by heavy-leaning political donors and with the indefatigable search by rafts of lawyers for loop-holes in the legislation, have made the protests of innocence louder and more arrogant without any serious concern for the harm to others and the society as a whole. It is here that corporate ethics becomes public ethics and the violations call for the rigour of the law as yet unknown in Ireland. It is here also that the calculating reason of corporate and public ethics and their translation into civil law require the assistance of the human imagination.

As we are in the middle of crisis it maybe useful to begin with the failures of imagination at work in the run up to it. The underlying belief in the power of the free market to correct itself, in the capacity of the invisible hand of the market to deliver prosperity to all, was a clear failure in imagination, a calculating blindness masquerading as reason. This was particularly true given the past histories of boom and bust and the more moderate views of such founders of the modern economic order as Adam Smith and John Maynard Keynes. Illuminating memory of past events and creative thinking about the future in any field is a function of the imagination. The concentration on trading money (speculating) instead of goods and services produced another blindness to the real economy, another failure in the imagination which led quickly to fiscal crisis and its now attendant and massive unemployment. Political attention to rescuing banks and bankers at the expense of employment and welfare for regular citizens shows how little 'little' people figure in the minds, the imaginations of our political and financial leaders, still heavily under the influence of growth at any cost. Such obsession with growth ignores the limitations of earthly resources, damages many of the earth's basics and leaves those who never gained that much from the boom having to pay disproportionately here, and still more in poorer countries, for the bust.

The fatal lack of imagination here, and it is fatal in the rising death-rate it causes directly through hunger, lack of health care, environmental damage and arms production, that fatal lack prevents the sympathy and empathy that puts people first, the more deprived and excluded people first of all. In moral and ethical terms people and their planetary environment must be more fully imagined to be more fully understood and so morally acceptable with equal rights and as of equal dignity. The discriminations still so widely and crudely practised in the economy, the law, the global society as a whole and even in what should be the primary repository of moral imagination and reason, the Christian church, betray ongoing imaginative and not just rational failures. The return of the imagination to economic and political discourse and practice in conjunction with reason is essential to overcoming the fractures in our local, national and global society and not just covering them up with more of the same while we await another bust with even worse of the same. What is called the common or community good, which the state, its laws and citizens are called to serve, is discerned by this combination of imagination and reason in discovering the real needs and aspirations of all the citizens and not the illusory and fantasy needs so often cultivated by politicians and corporate powers. The auguries are not at present promising but that uncalculating, poetic and Christian virtue of hope springs eternal. So with imagination, reason, vision and hope, an authentic corporate and public ethics may emerge.

Given the need for vision in one of the most deprived regions of our country in the midst of yet another economic crisis, let me conclude with an older Irish vision, poem and parable: *A Vision of Connaught in the Thirteethenth Century* by nineteenth century poet, James Clarence Mangan. (1861)

I walked entranced
Through a land of Morn
The sun with wondrous excess of light,
Shone down and glanced
Over sea of corn
And lustrous gardens aleft and right.
Even in the clime
Of resplendent Spain,
Beams no such sun upon such a land;
But it was the time,
'Twas in the reign
Of Cahal Mor of the Wine-red Hand.

CHAPTER TWO

'Inwardness' and the Economic Crisis

For Seamus Heaney at seventy

As reported in the United States, where I happened to be at the time, Seamus Heaney on his seventieth birthday, and in reply to questions on the value of poetry in the midst of economic crisis, said that it is just at such moments that people realise that they do not live by economics alone. 'If poetry and the arts can do anything, they can fortify your inner life, your inwardness', he said, 'and so act as a kind of "immune system" against material difficulties.' It may be a measure of the deservedly high standing of the poet, and of the current low standing of religious leaders, that I doubt that any bishop could have made a similar comment without attracting criticism. In fact I seem to remember, without being able to verify it when writing, that some bishop did so earlier in the crisis only to be immediately put down. If poets in Shelley's phrase are not yet 'the legislators' in the land, they may well be its spiritual directors. Although he would be the last to claim such a role in any traditional sense, Seamus Heaney is a huge and hugely positive spiritual influence in Ireland and further a field today. In that context it behoves Irish religious leaders and thinkers to attend to what he and other Irish poets and artists have to offer to the spiritual and moral, cultural and even economic renewal of our country. This brief reflection, prompted by the celebrations surrounding his birthday, may lead theologians and other believers to take seriously and interiorly the work of Heaney and his fellow artists.

Artists can be shrewd managers of their own business affairs and theologians have been known to drive hard bargains for salaries and lecture-fees, but by and large they are ignorant of the complexities of the financial world and innocent of its more shameful machinations. All of which means they have to tread very carefully in responding to the current crisis. In any event the

major causes and consequences have been so widely and sensa-
tionally presented in the media that it would be impossible for
anyone to be totally ignorant of or indeed personally unaffected
by them. When not just an economic crisis is raging but more
deeply a social crisis with all its destructive ramifications, poet
and priest may not sit on the sidelines. And what they have to
offer should reach towards the deeper moral and spiritual
malaise underlying Irish society as it moved almost inevitably
from boom to bust in economic terms and in record time.

While serious economic analysis exceeds the writer's competence and the regulation finger-pointing at the 'villains', from
politicians to bankers to developers to regulators, has been end-
lessly repeated, a few echoes of the tired 'defence of indefensible'
may be in order. Most blatantly misleading and morally bankrupt
were the common chants usually issued in quick succession: 'I
take full responsibility', 'I did nothing wrong', and 'It can't happen again' as someone else takes the blame or is even fired. (To be
fair this series has not been unknown in church circles either.) The
combination of greed, of recklessness with other people's money,
defrauding of accounts, denial of wrongdoing, attempts to cover
the fraud and evade tax, plus arrogant demands to be bailed out
by taxpayers whom they have already cheated, provide an exem-
plary list, and require for their assessment little enough economic
or moral expertise. They do, however, betray a nationwide culture which affects more than the economy or its power-brokers
and forces us back to examining the 'inwardness' of which
Heaney speaks.

Human inwardness is an embodied inwardness but none the
less inward for that. The embodied spirit that is the paradox of
human existence leads a double-single life .There is no inner,
spiritual activity in mind or heart that is not dependent on and
expressed in bodily terms, just as there is no external action of
movement that does not reflect some inner participation. All of
these interrelations are matters of degree and from a moral point
of view may be good or evil just as from a bodily point of view
they may be healthy or unhealthy.

For the poet as for the theologian the instrument of their art is the 'word'. Heaney, like all great poets, emerges from his immersion in world and words to give sound and vision to our deepest experiences. The path of this mysterious process is not easy to trace, not even for the poet himself. Various great poets have attempted to account for it in different ways. The rest of us can only receive, admire and reflect. Yet in reception and reflection we may recognise important aspects of the process and achievement, of the inward struggle and the final outward expression, inextricably bound as they are. One of the most precious aspects is the bond between the experience and its capture in the word, 'intimate' and 'exact' to invoke Heaney's language from a very different context ('Punishment'). The intimate and exact are far from the world of trade and economics. A close observer of his father as cattle-dealer, he knew enough of 'splitting the difference' and shaking on it to recognise the honesty and trust and so intimacy that touched such deals. The personal involvement and the honest man's word made for a respectable business despite the occasional rogue trader. *Caveat emptor*, let the buyer beware, usually remained far in the background. This honesty in dealing is rooted in that inner life we call *conscience* as it alerts and commands the values of truth and fairness or justice. The exact and intimate choice of word by the poet as he offers it to the reader is no less a demand of conscience. The ethics of poetry, as Eavan Boland and others have called it, is essential not only to good poetry but to healthy exchange within the good society. That such healthy and honest exchange was completely lost sight of in recent financial affairs is our everyday story and tragedy. We return to such exchange and its impact on society later. For now let us turn to another obsession of Heaney, its childhood roots and its relevance to the current crisis.

Object Lessons is the title of a fine book of literary criticism with a strong autobiographical touch by poet Eavan Boland. I borrow the title here for my own purposes in discussing Heaney's call to 'Inwardness' in economic bad times. In the *Cambridge Companion to Seamus Heaney*, published for his seventieth birthday, John Foster Wilson emphasises Heaney's preoccupation in his poetry with individual material objects, things, from the first poem in his first collection, ('pen, spade' from Digging in *Death of a Naturalist*) through 'A Hazel Stick for Catherine' and 'A Kite for Michael and Christopher' through a dozen other implements, trees, animals and fish.

These things of the material world become in Heaney's consciousness, words, poetry, things of the spirit too without ever losing the heft of the axe or gravity of the fifty-six pound weight. The poet's attunement to the material reveals his inwardness, his spirituality in ways akin to and perhaps derived from the Christian beliefs in Creation and Incarnation, however he understands these now. More interestingly for economic life, his attention to actual material goods, natural or manufactured, and so to their trade, exposes the weakness and eventual destructiveness of recent financial trading in the unreal goods of futures, sub-prime mortgages, hedge-funds, toxic assets-debts and all the other unintelligible ills the financial system and its words are heir to. Without its being rooted in world and work and subject to the bond of word given and word kept, without that spiritual ballast as the poet or theologian might put it, collapse is inevitable. 'Who steals my purse really steals trash.' In the current trashy world he may, in the white collar power of his caste, also leave me without job, income or pension; food, medicine or shelter, never to make recompense. Another material-spiritual casualty. And today we have 'quantitative easing'.

Beneath and through the tattered financial network lies the suffering human network which the poet's antennae discern and reveal. Heaney, in a lecture on Dylan Thomas, quotes Eavan Boland on the significance of tone in poetry and how that tone reflects a suffering undertow. It is a tone and an undertow characteristic of Heaney's best poetry as he grapples directly and indirectly with the tragedies of the Northern Troubles(Casualty and Station Island vii), of domestic loss (brother, 'Mid-Term Break'), mother ('Clearances vii', *et al*). What impresses this reader is how the pain of the loss is combined with the beauty of the expression without betraying either pain or beauty. There are also many marvellous instances of his ability to let the murderous and miraculous inhabit the same poem, in relation to the Troubles in particular, and to let the inwardness transform both,. In a world of unceasing conflict and recurrent natural disasters his permanent role as ambassador for the Republic of Conscience exposes once again the shallowness of so much of the justice talk and showy philanthropy of some 'billionaire exploiters and tax evaders'.

Without necessarily agreeing fully with John Montague's comment on 'Heaney's brooding devotion to the earth goddess', his nature poetry must be some of the most glorious of our time whether it deals with his native South Derry, his later attachment to Wicklow, the American prairie or western Irish coast. For compact observation of landscape and seascape and for beauty of word and image and music, 'Postscript' is many people's favourite.

Postscript
And sometime make the time to drive out west
Into County Clare, along the Flaggy Shore,
In September or October, when the wind
And the light are working off each other
So that the ocean on one side is wild
With foam and glitter, and inland among stones
The surface of a slate-grey lake is lit
By the earthed lightning of a flock of swans,
Their feathers roughed and ruffling, white on white,
Their fully grown headstrong-looking heads
Tucked or cresting or busy underwater.
Useless to think you'll park and capture it
More thoroughly. You are neither here nor there,
A hurry through which known and strange things pass
As big soft buffetings come at the car sideways
And catch the heart off guard and blow it open.

If there are any green shoots of recovery emerging in the present economic desert they well be rooted in the earth and its environment. But only if the climatic catastrophe that has been threatened for some time is averted by attending to the inward and transforming appreciation of nature which Heaney and others offer us. The health of the eco-system is undoubtedly essential to our physical survival, its beauty *à la* Heaney is essential to our cultural and spiritual survival,

There are many types of inwardness which Heaney explores and celebrates, at their climax in personal relations and community life. Best read these for oneself. In all his work the interaction between the aesthetic and the ethical, between the beautiful, the truthful and the good stands in serious judgement on the 'values', or better 'disvalues', manifested in our recent economic practices and supportive culture. Beyond that, they provide both education and inspiration in overcoming these disvalues in a fresh perspective and practice of the traditional 'transcendentals' as they were called, the true, the good and the beautiful. Heaney's attention to our Roman and Greek ancestors clearly makes him feel at home with such transforming realities.

His more immediate sources in his childhood Catholicism or ancient Irish Christianity are no less evident and even more influential. The Western Christian and classical association of religion and conscience with the good, the true and the beautiful in Aristotelian (Aquinas) or Platonic (Augustine) terms merges in and out of Heaney without finally revealing to this reader his ultimate commitment. However, like so many of his generation he inhabits several dimensions of inwardness or spirited bodiliness. Consciousness and conscience, discernment of right from wrong, senses of truth, goodness and beauty have already been noted. Does inwardness stop there for Heaney or other poets and artists? In their estimation the answer may be yes or no. For the religious believer and the theologian the answer is no, although not always without its hesitations. All of these inner dimensions reach toward a transcendence which cannot be either simply demonstrated or simply denied. Yet it can give a foundation, depth and fulfillment to the other dimensions which does not seem to be otherwise attainable. In the present shoddy ethical and spiritual crisis, that transcendence could prove the transforming power which is finally needed. It is already in preparation through the active inwardness of poets and artists, even by and for those who are unable or unwilling to recognise it .One recently deceased con-

temporary who did recognise it, if not without obscurities of his
own, was R. S. Thomas. His poem, *The Bright Field*, connects along
the biblical route with Heaney's comment, 'That people cannot
live by economics alone.' There is another treasure available for
those who have the eyes to see and the good judgement to go with
them.

> The Bright Field
> I have seen the sun break through
> to illuminate a small field
> for a while, and gone my way
> and forgotten it. But that was the pearl
> of great price, the one field that had
> the treasure in it. I realize now
> that I must give all that I have
> to possess it. Life is not hurrying
>
> on to a receding future, nor hankering after
> an imagined past. It is the turning
> aside like Moses to the miracle
> of the lit bush, to a brightness
> that seemed as transitory as your youth
> once, but is the eternity that awaits you.

The well educated entrepreneurs and bankers and larger
educated work-force of which we boasted before the bust did not
lack business know-how or technical competence. They did however lack Thomas's sense of perspective and Heaney's inwardness. We will have to work anew to regain them.

CHAPTER THREE

The Centrality of Justice

In Tribute to Patrick Hannon

In a new biblical fantasy world the 'Freedomites' would be at per-
petual war with the 'Justiceites' while the 'Shalomites' ('Peaceniks')
would be completely marginalised. And the Lords of the Western
World would provide the arms. Perhaps not that much of a fantasy,
as war is waged by the powerful in the name of freedom, without
any real reference to justice or international law. Anyway justice
today usually means control by the major economic powers with
at least the complicity of major and sometimes minor political
powers. Globalisation from above, sometimes promoted or en-
sured by the military sky-gods, remains the dominant force in the
modern world, while globalisation from below, from the powerless citizens of the world with all their theoretical equality in dignity, rights, freedom and justice, solidarity and peace, remain
mere raw material in themselves or in what they supply for the
current, self-appointed 'Masters of the Universe'.

In his theological and legal work, in service of students and
prisoners, Patrick Hannon combined his theological insights, his
legal and forensic skills and his elegant literary style to great effect. His earlier university studies in English literature and his
years teaching English have made him one of the most readable
writers of theology around. His doctoral studies in theology on
love and marriage in Augustine provided him with capacity for
critical and creative theological thought. His legal studies, leading
to his being called to the Irish Bar, gave him the legal knowledge
and precision which had been of such value to the Irish Episcopal
Commission for Prisoners Overseas. More recently he has been
writing clearly and effectively on issues of war and peace. In the
'real-fantasy' world of globalisation from the skies with scant regard for the earth or its inhabitants, Patrick Hannon has much to
offer to resisting peoples, resisting Christians and resisting theo-

logians. In accordance with the wishes of the Editor, this essay in his honour will concentrate on one of the focal points in his moral theology, justice. As practitioners of that discipline know only too well, it is impossible simply to separate justice from its 'natural' companions, freedom and peace, or from its Christian *fons et origo*, Love/Charity.

In moral discourse 'justice' is frequently regarded as the 'hard man' of the moral virtues. In religious discourse the justice of God may be used to terrify, with the God of the Hebrew scriptures in his punitive justice lazily contrasted with the God of Jesus Christ, the God of love who *is* Love. In Hebrew biblical terms the God of Israel is the God of creation, of promise/covenant and of forgiveness/reconciliation/renewal who is in a positive rather than punitive sense a God of justice and of loving-kindness, as their paralleling in the psalms among other historical, wisdom and prophetic writings affirms. All this is finally confirmed for New Testament readers and believers in Jesus' response to the query about which is the first commandment of the law, obviously the Mosaic Covenant Law. Loving God and your neighbour has its roots in that covenant but it becomes much more overt and central in the New Covenant established in the teaching, life, death and resurrection of the new Moses, Jesus Christ.

One way of illustrating this most effectively would be by comparing Moses' mountain charter, the Ten Commandments, with Jesus' mountain charter, the Sermon on the Mount (in Matthew as against Luke, with his Sermon on the Plain). Some reflection on and dialogue between these two central moral manifestos may help in discerning the basics of biblical morality and indeed of biblical justice. A third partner in the 'trialogue' would be that great, modern charter of Justice, the UN Declaration of Human Rights, 1948, with its antecedents and successors in various covenants, declarations and institutions.

The Ten Commandments were, as biblical scholars agree, the fruit of the interaction between different moral and religious traditions, and the existence of two different versions of the Sermon are found in the canonical gospels. Neither is it credibly claimed that either version represents as it stands the immediate composition of Jesus. The evangelists probably brought together from the oral traditions a series of connected insights and sayings attributable in various ways to Jesus, if not all utterly original. However the Ten Words, as they are sometimes called, have a history after as well as before they were written down, and in the Christian church as well as in the later scriptures, commentaries and life of the people of the Mosaic Covenant, so that they are one of the truly formative moral influences in the wider Western world.

The Manuals which dominated Catholic Moral Theology from the Council of Trent to the Second Vatican Council devoted one large volume to the Ten Commandments, with justice treated, rather narrowly it must be admitted, under the seventh commandment, 'Thou shalt not steal'. As an alternative, particularly in manuals produced by the Dominicans, the virtues took precedence over the commandments in organisation, but in practical terms the virtue model moved very little beyond the treatment of justice under the rubric of the seventh commandment. However, of the Sermon on the Mount there was not a whisper in the manuals of either kind. That belonged not to the moral teaching of the church but to its counsels of perfection and 'spiritual' reading and direction, in so far as it figured at all outside the commentaries on the gospels in Scripture Studies. In fact the only New Testament reference in such moral theology was to Jesus' comments on divorce in the volume / section dealing with the sixth and ninth commandments. This was a separate volume for example in the Noldin-Schmidt manual, while marriage was treated in the volume on the sacraments and as with the other sacraments almost exclusively in canon law terms. Noldin-Schmidt remained a standard textbook well into the 1960s.

Moral Theology and the Medievals
In many scholars' estimation, including that of the distinguished moral theologian, Bernard Häring, the introduction of private penance by the Irish monks in the seventh and eighth centuries and their composition and circulation of (Irish) penitentials had a very negative, long-term effect on the development of moral

theology. In that view, moral theology was focused on sinful acts as matter for Confession. This was also reflected in the *Summae Confessariorum* of the High Middle Ages which eventually issued in the post-Trent manuals which were really textbooks for confessors to be used in the new, reformed training of priests. All this was compounded by the rapid development of Canon Law from the twelfth century on. Canon Law influenced the development of moral theology in two important ways. Moral obligations tended to be thought of more and more as legal obligations and more obligations of Christian living were in fact those of church or Canon Law. By the time of the manuals, in the volume on the sacraments for example most of the matter considered was church law. The treatment of justice in this context focused on acts of injustice between individuals such as stealing another's property without any attention to deeper personal issues such as the personal virtue of justice or broader social issues such as poverty and power in the context of what would now be called structural justice or injustice.

A very different strand of 'moral theology' was developing at this time also, with the discovery of the Greek philosophers, particularly of Aristotle, and their influence on theologians. In terms of theological achievement at the time and of subsequent and continuing influence, St Thomas Aquinas was the key figure. It should be noted that he and his peers never used the term 'moral theology' and did not really have our distinctions of disciplines between scripture, dogmatic and moral theology. Theology was a single enterprise for them, embracing all the disciplines we now distinguish. Admittedly Thomas did treat ethical or moral issues within the *Secunda Pars* of his *Summa*, with basic issues such as the *'lex aeterna Dei'* which included the *lex naturalis* and *lex nova* in the *Prima Pars* of the *Secunda Pars*. It should also be made clear that he sharply distinguished and separated *lex Dei* and its components from *lex humana*, whether of church (*lex canonica*) or of state (*lex civilis*). Moral as distinct from legal issues came under the *lex Dei*. In another significant move continuing his dialogue between Christianity and other traditions, as well as between Augustine and Aristotle, he distinguished the *lex nova* as founded in Christ and his revelation, which he described as inscribed in the heart of the Christian by the presence of the Holy Spirit.

It is this presence which integrates and transforms the moral virtues of the broader traditions, even the cardinal or hinge virtues as Aristotle and Aquinas call them, justice, courage, temperance and prudence, so that charity becomes the form of all the virtues. This is taken to mean that the activities proceeding from the moral virtues are, for the Christian, expressions of what Jesus called the first and second commandments, love of God and love of neighbour. In the further insight of John's letter, they express God's self who is love, inscribed in our hearts, forming New Commandment, New Covenant, indeed in Pauline terms New Creation. It is in this incarnational and redemptive context with its transformative force that the role of justice in theological ethics or moral theology may be properly understood and explicated without undermining the central secular and humanistic value of justice as frequently invoked and applied in our Western world, if not always given adequate analysis or foundation. The various past and current theories of justice as affecting individual relations or entering into the moral formation of society have much to contribute to moral theology as well as to moral philosophy and to their value in enlightening the practice of justice. From Plato and Aristotle to Augustine and Aquinas, from Luther and Calvin to Barth, from Kant to Macintyre and Rawls, to select names almost at random, complementary and conflicting strands of the Christian and human theory/virtue/practice of justice have striven for recognition and integration. In this brief essay in theological ethics, much of that must be taken for granted and some few strands isolated in search for an exposition of justice as significant to the discipline in which Patrick Hannon has so distinguished himself, contemporary Catholic moral theology.

Creation, Differentiation and Justice
The return to creation as a primary theological and indeed ethical resource for Christian theologians is overdue but developing quite quickly. More disputable but equally valuable is the overcoming of the discontinuity between creation and redemption

and so between the God of the Old Testament or Covenant and the God of the New Testament or Covenant, indeed in Paul's phrase, of the New Creation. And all this has important implications for justice in moral theology.

In the Genesis and other biblical accounts, the Creator God is depicted as making and observing the universe as distinct from, differentiated from Godself. 'God made the heavens and the earth ... and saw that they were good.' In this vision of creation both the differentiation and so the difference or otherness of the created world is at once established and recognised / respected as good, given its due in justice, as later moral terminology might put it. Simultaneously by these biblical accounts the universe itself is progressively differentiated, from the division into light and dark, ocean and dry land, through the different plants and animals to the critical differentiation of humans from the rest of the world ('And God saw that (they) were very good') and their differentiation as male and female individuals. At the level of human creation and differentiation, human justice in response to God (religion) and in response to one another becomes possible and mandatory as does human respect for the wider world in their stewardship of it. Aquinas picks up on this when he categorises religion as a subcategory of the cardinal virtue of justice. Contemporary writer George Steiner provides a striking Genesis-related image of human beings as 'Guests of Creation'. In all these visions and versions it is important to remember that creation is not a once for all completed divine action but a continuing activity of the Creator-God who remains engaged with humanity and the world, as the Hebrew and Christian scriptures attest.

The justice of God in relation to creatures expresses the divine recognition of and commitment to their created worth and goodness as differentiated and in that sense set over against, other than, God's self. Where human creatures fail to live up to this worth and goodness and so fail to respond as they should, they are themselves guilty of injustice and incur the judgement of God. This judgement, which is frequently mentioned in both Old and New Testament, testifies to the reality of the differentiation, the freedom of humans and the authentic justice of God. Yet as noted above it is a justice set within a richer divine reality. In the history of Israel it is sometimes combined with that characteristic of God which in Hebrew is called *hesed*, meaning loving kindness as in Psalm 85 etc. The movement in the book by minor prophet Zephaniah from extended condemnatory judgement of all creation, including Judah and Jerusalem, by their God to merciful renewal, is typical of so much of the whole Hebrew corpus. And the two great commands of the New Testament, love of God and love of neighbour, are already clearly proclaimed in the Old. In both testaments, then, justice in the relationship between Creator and creatures is clearly demanded, yet contained within the overarching reality of love while lacking the equality which Aristotle thought crucial to strict justice. Justice between human beings themselves is an intrinsic component of both testaments and with serious attention to justice for the poor and marginalised. Indeed for Jeremiah, to do justice is to know God and for Amos, neglect and exploitation of the weak renders worship of God futile. This attention to people on the margins is so characteristic of Jesus' ministry and teaching that it becomes the basis for final divine judgement in Matthew 25, for example. Yet it is justice and judgement in the context of the overriding power of the God who is love.

Guests of Creation
Before moving into some of the regular concerns of justice in moral theology which are normally confined to human relationships, both personal and social, it may be helpful to reflect a little further on the human condition as creature within a much larger creation as gift of the Creator-God. George Steiner's phrase does not necessarily include the recognition of such a divine Creator, although in such books as *Real Presences* and *Grammar of Creation*, he comes very close to it. However, I adopt the phrase to my own rather than his purposes, and without attributing such belief to him, I use it as expressing my own belief that as guests of creation we humans are also guests of the Creator. For a Christian theologian this is an obvious move with important moral implications for our whole lives and for the moral reality of justice. As indicated

above, equality on which many theories and practices of justice depend does not apply as between God and creatures, even human creatures. Yet the Jewish and Christian traditions emphasise the justice of God in dealing with human beings but always tempered by loving mercy and forgiveness because of human limitations and failures. Mercy and forgiveness will also be seen to be a feature of just relationships between equals (i.e. humans) even if it has been neglected or ignored in much discussion of justice in moral theology and moral philosophy. The creature-hood of humans has other important implications which have often been distorted in theological circles by reducing human beings to blind obedience to divine commands as mediated by scripture without due regard (in justice) for the proper processes of interpretation or the appropriate free response of human beings. As against the blind obedience error, the recognition of human creature-hood helps prevent the promethean reach to unlimited power by individuals or groups, which is always at the expense of other individuals or groups and so unjust. History records many horrific instances of this overreaching in power and the consequent injustices, while today's news bulletins carry endless examples in destructive economic and political dominance.

A more subtle but no less destructive consequence of ignoring human creature-hood and our position as guests and not lords of creation, is human treatment of planet earth as simply humanity's own to dominate and exploit. There is a tradition of using Genesis 1:28 to justify human domination of the earth, often accompanied by accusations against Christianity of justifying the 'rape of the earth'. That would certainly be an exaggeration. However, the overall biblical view of all animate and inanimate creation as reflecting God's glory and eliciting God's care offers a very different vision, of human beings as guests, admirers and stewards of creation, who, at the same time as they cherish the earth, must with restraint live off it. Christianity then encourages an enjoyment of the earth's beauty, justice to its differentiated elements and a loving care for them by human beings set within the divine gift of creation. Too many even Christian defenders of ethics towards the environment rely too heavily on utilitarian arguments about

the need to protect the earth's resources for the use of the present
and future human generations, without reflecting on and respect-
ing its own beauty, mystery and integrity. Others reduce humans
to being just one other species, removing the possibility of a true
aesthetic and moral let alone religious response.

The final and perhaps most important challenge in this section
is to differentiate the dignity and worth of human beings as essential to their equality by their all sharing in the divine dignity, without making them into god-lings themselves, with all the power
struggles and injustice that would involve towards one another
and the environment, and without making morality and justice,
including human rights, into some simply human, even arbitrary
and perhaps disposable invention. For Jews and Christians, root-
ing of human dignity in the divine gives each human being an
equal and irreducible character as a secure basis for both their personal rights and responsibilities, including their responsibilities
to the wider creation.

The Hard Core of Morality, Christian and Human

Encounters between Creator and creatures, between humans and
their fellows reveal the irreducible differences which exist between them and the (moral) demand to recognise and respect
these differences. To fail to do so by ignoring or seeking to possess
the other is in the vision of Emmanuel Levinas to 'murder them'.
(We leave aside for the moment the encounters and relationships
between humans and non-human creatures.) Levinas, like some
modern philosophers / theologians, emphasises the human (and
divine) other as the source and summons of morality. Without following him or others to the letter, it seems clear that moral call and
response emerge in such encounters and are sustained in the continuing relationships within which people live, with one another
and with their God. At the centre of such moral encounters and relationships is the summons to respect one another as persons in
their irreducible differences, in their needs and gifts, in their rights
and responsibilities. This is the hard core of morality, giving to
one another our basic due of recognition and respect and responding to their particular need, exercising the virtue of justice to all.

From acceptance of this hard core of justice came the recognition of natural rights, later rights of man and now human rights, which play a key role in seeking to establish just societies and a just world. The United Nations' Declaration of Human Rights with its associated covenants and conventions, such as the European Convention, provide a basic platform for the promotion and protection of justice between and within countries. And despite gross violations of such rights, even in countries of their birth and development, they are an indispensable instrument of national and international politics and law in the pursuit of justice. Given the rigours of their formulation, their development in reach and application and their growing incorporation in law at national and international levels, human rights are one of humanity's great moral discoveries and achievements. In the Western tradition, from which in their modern form they emerged, they rank with the Jewish Decalogue and the Christian Sermon on the Mount as major shapers of our moral universe. Yet they do not and cannot stand alone. As many critics have observed, rights must always be balanced by accompanying responsibilities. While some of these critics may be defending their own or others' privileges, power and possessions against the deprived claiming their rights, an integral justice will combine regard for the responsibilities of all with priority for the claims of those deprived of basic human rights and freedoms. The whole inhabited world bears witness to the difficulties of such combination. In Ireland we are still wrestling with such conflicting claims in Northern Ireland, with new conflicts over immigrants and asylum seekers and, apparently the most intractable of all, those between the settled community and the traveller community.

A different form of criticism of the emphasis on human rights emerges from their perception and sometimes their exercise in purely individual terms. Despite the recognition of cultural, social and economic rights in the original charter and particular covenants, their Western provenance and dominant Western individualism have frequently restricted human rights to the political rights of individuals in society. Development of rights transcending the simply individual is in progress although there is a

long way to go. Apart from that, human rights cannot stand alone
as the only bearers of morality between individuals and societies.
Even the addition of responsibilities corresponding to each right
would not provide an adequate framework for truly moral and
human relationships and societies. Marriage, for example, must
take seriously reciprocal rights and responsibilities but it needs
more than that. So do so many other human relationships and institutions, moral values and practices. Without a basis in justice
and so in rights and responsibilities, families and friendships,
local communities and schools, churches and voluntary bodies
from sporting organisations to justice-seeking NGOs and political
parties themselves could not survive. To thrive as human realities
they need generosity and self-sacrifice, compromise, forgiveness
and reconciliation and other moral practices which cannot be
neatly pigeon-holed under rights, with or without the add-on of
responsibilities. Justice itself is a larger word than rights even in
the current secular language of morality. In the Jewish and
Christian traditions, as we have seen, it connects easily with loving-kindness and mercy on God's side and with religion and worship on the human side.

Justice and Forgiveness

As the hard core of morality, justice implies a strictness that might
easily slip into unnecessary harshness. More dangerously, it might
be pursued in a vengeful manner that precludes the possibility of
restoring the human relations, whose violation was clearly an
offence against justice, between individuals or within society or
both. The pursuit of justice through the courts, the compensation
for the injury caused and, if necessary for the safety of society and
the rehabilitation of the offender, the imprisonment of the con-
victed, is not in purely human terms the end of the affair. The full
human resolution lies in the restoration of relations between offended and offender and between offender and society. This involves for the injured party the completion of justice, the render-
ing of his due to the other in the traditional definition, by forgiveness which can only result in reconciliation, the restoration of true
human relationships by the return, repentance, conversion of the

offending other. If this is rare in the practice of criminal or other
forms of justice, it may be because it is ignored in moral, civic and
legal education. In theological education there is no excuse for its
omission. At the practical level of the sacrament of penance, forgiveness and restoration of relationship with God and community
are central. In the biblical understanding of justice as we have
seen, it is closely related to mercy and so to forgiveness. The dynamic justice of God as expressed in continuing divine creation
has forgiveness at its leading edge, as God seeks to renew or restore right(-eous) relationships with creatures. As Christians we
pray each day as taught by Jesus, 'Our father ... forgive us our
trespasses as we forgive those who trespass against us.' Jesus' forgiving his enemies on the Cross remains our teacher and model.
For the just man who falls seven times every day forgiving seventy
times seven seems hardly excessive. And we have in personal experience or in the media our regular human models amidst the
domestic and political conflicts which afflict us. For Irish consolation and inspiration, Gordon Wilson's forgiveness of the killers
of his daughter who died as he held her hand was deeply significant. Only by combing justice with such forgiveness will reconciliation and peace be restored as Mohandas Gandhi, Martin Luther
King, Nelson Mandela and so many others knew so well.

Freedom, Justice and Peace

In developing and teaching moral theology, a series of difficult
dialogues between theory and practice, between sacred and secular
traditions and many others is required. One of the more useful
dialogues for addressing social issues may be between the Jewish-
Christian vision of Freedom, Justice and Peace and the modern
triad of Liberty, Equality and Fraternity. As I have attempted this
at some length elsewhere, (*The Gracing of Society*, Dublin 1990), I
will concentrate on the biblical vision and its development here
while keeping the terms associated particularly with the French
Revolution in the background. In the order presented here, justice
is placed between freedom and peace and not by accident but by
theology. The freedom of the Creator was primary and was
shared with human creatures from their beginning. The different-

iation between Creator and creatures involved the recognition and respect for difference and its demands which are called justice, divine justice and human justice. Such justice could only be freely and fully exercised in community, in reconciling relationships, in peace. The kiss of justice and peace as envisioned in Psalm 85 may be never more than partially realised in history but it is the goal towards which all human beings are called to strive. The blessed justice-seekers and blessed peace-makers of the Sermon on the Mount must eventually freely include all humankind, believing and unbelieving alike. Of such is the kingdom of God for such is God. The ultimate divine mystery of the Triune God might be briefly if crudely invoked here in its distinctive persons as the freely creating Father, the justifying Son and the bonding and peace-making Spirit. At least the moral theologian may never evade that unifying and differentiating mystery, however deeply s/he must enter into the tangled undergrowth of human relations, rights and responsibilities.

Globalisation and the Reign of God

Of the moral dialogues referred to above, for theologians and above all moral theologians who focus on justice, the most important may be that between the current phenomena of globalisation and the present and eschatological realisation of the kingdom or reign of God. Once again I excuse myself from any extended discussion as I have already treated the subject at some length in the publication on Globalisation in the series *Christian Perspectives on Development* (Veritas/Trócaire/Cafod, Dublin, 2005). However the connection between these two great symbols, of the secular and sacred respectively, and their realisation, partially and ambiguously in both cases I believe, puts great strain on the moral practices and theories of justice. For too many people, religious or no, globalising, as I prefer to call it, is purely a matter of economics and technology. Add in the dominant ideology of the free market and globalising readily becomes economic colonialism, even imperialism. The threatened reduction of all the peoples and cultures of the world to economic units and processes at the bidding of powerful corporations and states is too awful to contemplate and will in any case meet with stiff resistance. The struggle for economic justice is world-wide and is gradually intensifying. Guideline for such a justice will depend on the vision and will of many partners including grassroots victims of the present process as well as NGOs, trade unions, corporations who are not simply driven by greed and can also see how self-interest may be served by more just arrangements for trade and aid in what must eventually become much more of a globalising from the bottom up. At the same time due respect must be accorded to different cultural and religious traditions where they do not obviously offend justice themselves. All this requires economic, political, cultural and religious dialogue of a kind that will promote a more free, just and peaceful world, thus realising something of the Christian vision of the reign of God.

CHAPTER FOUR

The Realism of Forgiveness and Its Risks

Remembering Una O'Higgins O'Malley

In the deepest layers of one's being there is hurt: hurt inflicted on self by self, hurt inflicted on self by others, leaving aside the totally accidental physical hurt for which no one is responsible and to which the themes of personal or political forgiveness do not directly apply. In conventional discussion the term 'forgiveness' has a soft, weak ring. Only the unforgiving are strong and retaliation is the symbol of that strength. In personal as in political conflict the weakest still go to the wall and the forgiving are readily identified as the weakest. At best they may be regarded as idealistic or innocent of the ways of the world, while their counterpunching counterparts proudly bear the standard of realism. And so it has been in most of our conflict-ridden and war-torn world from Homer's *Iliad* to Kavanagh's *Epic*. As so often, in Flannery O'Connor's phrase, the violent bear it away; forgiveness becomes no more than an illusion and a dangerous, even suicidal one at that, certainly in political contexts.

There are other ways of reading and writing the same history, be it personal or political. The academic adage that history is written by the victors is seldom invoked to challenge a particular victorious interpretation. There are, of course, notable and recurring exceptions – in the context of various Irish conflicts, the slogan that it is not those who can inflict the most (suffering/hurt) who are the ultimate winners but those who can endure the most. This endurance did not, of course, necessarily include forgiveness but forgiveness does require some capacity for endurance, while continued infliction of hurt excludes the exercise of and perhaps the capacity for forgiveness. Unforgiving and unforgiven persons are defective human beings. Although it is not necessarily their fault, they are both lacking in the health and wholeness of integral humanity. This deficiency might seem more obviously culpable

in the case of the unforgiving but the unforgiven may also be contributors to their condition in their unwillingness to seek or accept
forgiveness. To understand the reality of forgiveness in its realism
and its risks, it is important to consider not only its personal
dimensions, critical as they are, but also its sociopolitical dimensions, its religious and inter-religious dimensions and, for Christians
at least, its eschatological and divine dimensions.

Divine Forgiveness
It may be more interesting and illuminating to begin with divine
forgiveness as recorded in the Hebrew and Christian scriptures,
not least because of the paradoxes that its various exercises present. The unconditional, free and gracious gift of the loving and all
merciful God embodies a demanding call for repentance, return,
conversion of mind and heart and lifestyle from the would-be forgiven human sinners, whether individual Israelites, the inhabitants of the particular cities of Tyre and Sidon or the whole people
of Israel. The graciousness of the forgiver, indeed the gratuitous-
ness of the actual forgiving, and the demands made of the forgiven
may seem an odd, if not contradictory, couple. The contradiction
is partly relieved in the case of divine forgiveness by the recognition that the repentance, the human response to the divine offer, is
also divine grace and gift. Although this is more obvious to us
through the history of Jesus than through the recorded history of
Israel. In Yahweh's fidelity to his promises and in their realisation
through Jesus Christ in what Paul describes as New Creation,
both the initiative and implementation of the project of forgiveness and salvation belong primarily and finally to the Creator and
Redeemer God.

The free availability of such divine forgiveness and at the same
time its ultimate costliness is revealed and realised in the ministry, life and death of Jesus Christ. His teaching and exercise of
forgiveness at the Sermon on the Mount and his forgiveness of his
executioners on the Mount of Golgotha indicate the divine and
human price to be paid by the forgiver. The self-emptying into
death of the Son of God in forgiving response as way to the New
Creation and New Humanity, Pauline parallels (Romans 5) to

Genesis 1 and 2, expose the depth of the recipient response called for from the forgiven. The disintegration of creaturely revolt with its matching disintegration of loving Creator on the cross provides the opening to resurrection for Jesus, the New Human, and for humanity as the New Creation. Enabled to die with him in repentance and to rise with him in forgiveness, humanity is fully healed, restored, even transformed. The trusting self-humiliation of the forgiving God is the model for repentant and, within its own circle, forgiving humanity.

Human Forgiveness
In the problematic dualities that afflict all human relationships as gift and threat to one another, as companion and competitor, enjoying and resenting, serious offence may be given and taken whoever's the fault. The consequences can reach from the trivial to the lethal with bitter and long-lasting estrangement between individuals, families and neighbours. Within marital and family relationships, in neighbourhoods and in social and charitable organisations, in religious institutions and political parties, the offence and division emerge sometimes in deeply hurtful fashion and the prospects of overcoming them can be very remote.

   Forgiveness does not come easily to most human beings, although co-existence short of true forgiveness and real reconciliation can make living together with such difficult differences tolerable for much of the time. There are always notable exceptions, often modelled among Christians on the words and example of Jesus. There were many such during the Northern Ireland killings, although not all were publicly known. The most striking example of that era was probably Gordon Wilson, who held the hand of his dying daughter Marie at the Remembrance Day bombing in Enniskillen in 1987 while forgiving the killers. Una O'Higgins O'Malley spent a lifetime promoting such forgiveness and organised a memorial Mass for her father and his killers on the fiftieth anniversary of his murder. For Gordon Wilson and Una O'Higgins O'Malley, their Christian faith played an explicit and acknowledged role, as no doubt it did for the many other forgiving deceased and bereaved in Northern Ireland and around

the world. The great twentieth-century apostles of non-violence
among the racially excluded and oppressed, Mohandas [Mahatma]
Gandhi, Martin Luther King and Nelson Mandela, owed much of
their charisma and effectiveness to their ability to forgive their enemies in the Spirit of Jesus. Beyond the world of political violence,
in the quarrels and violence that surface in domestic and other
small-scale circles, human forgiveness is no less necessary, no less
difficult and no less exceptional. The spouses or the brothers or
the neighbours or the colleagues who have not spoken for years
remain trapped in the unforgiving deep freeze. Appeals simply to
Jesus' way is seldom effective in initiating, still less completing,
the defrosting process. Human forgiveness may be finally, if
anonymously, fuelled by the Spirit of God but the human spirit
has its own journey, long or short, to discern and to travel from
paralysing resentment and rejection of the offending other to appreciation and acceptance of that other. The process of forgiveness is only completed by the mutual acceptance and appreciation of offender and offended.

In Truth and Justice
In mutual acceptance and appreciation, truth must be acknowledged and justice done, however difficult both these may be for
the participants. But it should be a loving truth, a truth discerned
in love, the divine love that embraces offender and offended, a
comprehensive love that takes account of the inevitable weaknesses and failures on both sides, however blatant in the circumstances those of the primary offender may be. Justice and its doing
is no less an essential component of forgiveness but it should be a
generous justice as of the forgiving God, where vindictiveness has
no place in the mind of the offended and evasion of rightful due is
no ambition of the offender. Again, the thrust of forgiveness with
its mutual acceptance will make such difficulties much more
manageable than, for example, a simple assertion or denial of
rights could. At least in that dynamic of forgiveness and repentance the deeper capacity of each party is called into play and their
deeper and more holistic relationship is realised. It is in the healed
and fuller relationships of the forgiving and the forgiven that the

new and richer realism is achieved, if never perfectly, as against the seriously defective realism of continuing enmity and bitterness.

Social and Political Forgiveness
So much that is spoken and written of forgiveness focuses on one-to-one personal relationships. With all its attendant difficulties for forgiver and forgiven, often of social and political background as already indicated, personal forgiveness can and does work – but not always, of course. Between social and political groups the difficulties increase to such a degree that they become for many protagonists and commentators of a different kind, so that these no longer wish to speak of forgiveness at all. This would appear to be confirmed by the frequently frozen character of group hurt, resentment, rejection and guilt. The ice-breaking that could initiate forgiveness and reconciliation may not be now, or in the foreseeable future, available.

For all the forbidding counter-examples, history does occasionally rhyme with hope of peace, reconciliation, even forgiveness. In the twentieth century, that most destructive of centuries, and in Europe, that most destructive of continents, from the horrors of Auschwitz and Stalingrad, from the rubble of Coventry and Dresden, there emerged a growing integration between the ancient enemies of Western Europe, now balanced precariously in face of the ominous threat of the USSR and its satellites. And then without a shot being fired the great symbolic wall of division in Berlin collapsed and all of Europe was suddenly exposed to the prospects of citizen freedom and inter-nation peace – not all accomplished as yet but so much beyond the hopes of even the most optimistic just twenty years ago. The reconciliation fostered in and by the European Union has had its implicit and explicit forgiving moments and symbols, actions and personalities, as Chancellor Brandt of Germany, for example, sought forgiveness from the Poles and a variety of nations and religions accepted their responsibility for the genocide of the Jews.

In the oft-despised continents of Africa and Asia, such insights came earlier in the century and clearer in their intent. Mohandas

Gandhi began his nonviolent campaign in South Africa for freedom, justice and peace for its oppressed peoples and by solely
nonviolent and peaceful means at the end of the nineteenth century.
Through the first half of the twentieth, he developed his political
analysis and liberating peace-making techniques in his native
India. In theory and practice, Gandhi offered the world ways of
political reconciliation and, by implication, forgiveness that have
still to be properly recognised and implemented by Western
powers. His most significant Western disciple was Martin Luther
King, the African American leader of the Civil Rights Movement
in the 1950s and 1960s who, like Gandhi, was assassinated for his
efforts. In Africa there emerged the towering figure of Nelson
Mandela who, despite universal expectations of a bloodbath in
the struggle against the apartheid government of South Africa,
enabled a peaceful transition of power. The subsequent Truth and
Reconciliation Commission presided over by Mandela's religious
associate Archbishop Desmond Tutu, for all the limitations of its
achievements, did present a very clear pattern of acknowledge-
ment and confession, repentance and remorse and reconciliation
and forgiveness unparalleled in modern politics. Its abuse or evasion by many guilty participants cannot diminish its significance
in the development of a politics of reconciliation and forgiveness.

Politics, even in its most secular practices, must eventually acknowledge past destructiveness and those whom it most affected.
In the deep heart's core of all civilised relationships between peoples and nations, the need for confession, repentance and forgiveness, however much stripped of their religious overtones, will
recur. In 2007, perhaps fresh expressions will help thaw some present frozen connections as well as remembering the need for liberating forgiveness in relation to the slave trade of past centuries
and its new manifestations in human trafficking today.

With these African, Asian and African American examples in
mind, it is difficult to depress the claims of such forgiving politics
to an authentic human reality in their consequences and an authentic human realism in their programmes. Of course, there
were risks, as all three examples amply illustrate. But would the
alternative of violence and war have posed fewer risks to op-

pressed and oppressor, their individual lives and community existence? And how realistic would the war alternative have been for the particular oppressed in search of liberation and for the particular oppressors in the longer term? And how authentically and really human would the post-victory and -defeat relationships have been for the victorious or defeated. In her insights into the futility of such violent military victories and defeats for both sides, Una O'Higgins O'Malley drew together her Irish experience and her Christian faith in ways that were closer to Mandela, King and Gandhi, who also cherished the nonviolent ways of Jesus, than to her patriotic forebears, even her father whom she rightly cherished so deeply.

By remembering to forgive and forgive and forgive, she helped move Irish people of all persuasions towards being a forgiving and a forgiven people.

CHAPTER FIVE

Strangers in Communion: Reflecting on Christian Marriage

For Hubert and Aldegonde Brenninkmeier

The founding of The International Association for Marital Spirituality (Intams) itself, and its integration of so many diverse strangers into a community over the years, are at once an example of the new community (*kaine koinonia*) which St Paul enunciated as the fruit of Christ's resurrection, and an expanded model of the communion of husband and wife which the Epistle to the Ephesians envisaged as an expression of the unity of Christ and his church. If one may be allowed a more personal note, intimacy and hospitality of such community and communion became evident to many of us over time in the relationship and hospitality of Hubert and Aldegonde. Theology always needs the personal note of experience, especially when discussing such a personal matter as marriage. For those of us who have not had the experience of marriage itself, the friendship of our married friends enables us in a limited way to share some human and Christian insight into the life and sacrament. In this short essay I wish to take a slightly more distant approach to human relationships in general and then move through further reflection on friendship to the intimacy of marriage itself. However, this should not suggest some simple linear progression as different relationships, friendships and marriages may emerge at different stages for different people.

The key to good human relationships is the move from the unknown to the known, from the stranger to the friend, from the feared to the loved. Again these are not straightforward, sustainable and permanent moves. For all kinds of inculpable as well as culpable reasons, from death and distance to jealousy and property, they may break down. At their best and persistent they will have their tensions and estrangements and require some at least minor mediations and reconciliations. These will be, or should be, the mediations and reconciliations of growth. For a fuller grasp of the dynamics of these persisting relationships it is necessary to begin where all relationships begin, even that most intimate one of mother and child, with the encounter of two complete strangers.

In the Genesis account of creation the divine power distinguishes the first humans as man and woman derived from the same stock and given to one another in a bonding love. Their subsequent estrangement from each other (they saw that they were naked and covered themselves) and from God (from whom they hid themselves) and the climax of that human estrangement in the Cain and Abel story, expresses Israel's effort to account for the history of human estrangement from God and one another in face of their faith in a loving Creator God. Our contemporary world and church is riddled with estrangements, hostile divisions between individuals, parties and nations. Yet the starting point of this reflection is not on the hostility but on actual separation and difference between individuals which anticipates the development of either hostile or friendly relations and has the potential for either. In an earlier expression exploring this area, I describe the other or stranger as both gift and threat with the potential to enrich or diminish. Indeed adopting the description 'other' as well as 'stranger' enables a more subtle analysis of one-to-one relationships.

A central feature of most human lives, perhaps of most living things, is fear of the unknown. For the sub-human certainly it is part of their strategy of survival. It may play a similar role in the development of human beings, but because they are educable in such rich and diverse ways they learn to circumvent the fear and to get to know the unknown. Yet this can be a slow and difficult process. However much progress is made, the bulk of the unknown remains unknowable to the individual human being and in cosmic terms to the human race as a whole. And that is the case whether you exclude or include a divine creator. This may come as a shock to some worshippers of scientific knowledge and its apparently indefinite range. They ignore or do not understand the limited nature of the knowledge which science provides even of the wonders of the atom and the tulip, and above all of the human person in all its dimensions and relationships. Human persons in relationship are the primary concern here and little enough expertise is needed to remind us of how little we know of the self not to speak of the other (person).

As indicated earlier all human relationships begin between strangers, between spouses, between parents and children, between friends, between work colleagues and neighbours. Not only do relationships begin between strangers, they continue, if they continue at all, between strangers. Indeed emerging strangeness is a condition of developing, healthy relationships. The more intimate the relationship is, the more the mutual strangeness emerges to provide new bases for closer mutual understanding and deeper bonding. Of course such new strangeness has also its element of threat and where the persons in relationship have not the determination and the ability to transform the potential threat into mutual enrichment the relationship is at risk. Too many marriage break-ups seek explanation in the mantra: 'This is not the person I married five, ten or even twenty years ago.' Of course not. Effective pre-marriage education should have emphasised that prospect of change. Continuous marriage support during difficulty should make it clear that the partners change and continue to change in ways that are potentially enriching but may prove on occasion seriously threatening. Without change and adaptation to it there is no growth and without growth there is only boredom or worse unto death. The ability to recognise and celebrate the fresh enriching strangeness in the other is the secret of all fulfilling relationships including marriage.

Meeting with the stranger or other person is often in practice a mixture of projection of the self, its characteristics and interests and genuine encounter with the other as other. Where projection dominates, the self is basically self-enclosed and unable to recognise the other as truly strange, as irreducibly and unpossessably other. This irreducible otherness is essential to true recognition of, respect for and authentic response to the other. It is an acceptance that the other simply transcends the self and may never become its possession or some kind of extension of the self or simply used for self-benefit. For the philosopher Emmanuel Levinas this is the beginning of ethics, which for him is also the beginning of philosophy (and theology). The self-transcendence and self-surrender involved in such serious encounter is for him provoked by the exterior reality of the other and in that sense anti-symmetric, of itself not demanding a return. Of course the self is also an other who provokes the stranger-other (the original self in our diagram) in similar fashion. That other may not respond to the provocation or to such transcendence, and so the relationship remains one-sided, permanently non-mutual. However, in living encounters the self-transcendence operates both ways and provides the basis for development of unity in difference. Such unity in difference has many expressions and varying degrees between neighbours, friends, work-colleagues, acquaintances, chance encounters and even media presences.

However, its potentially profoundest, closest and most lasting human expression is in marriage, where it might be more aptly described as strangers in communion, one-flesh communion. The very one-flesh description with its deeper mind-spirit dimensions reveals and emphasises the reality of the communion. Yet that coming together in surrender is necessarily succeeded by separation into the distinct others in which both may be transformed in part by the experience of such unity. The dynamics of union and separation, not just in bodily union and separation but in the daily communal living in the home or at work, follow the patterns of self-transcendence in surrender to the stranger becoming obviously more familiar as the couple grow together. Yet the fresh strangeness, which such familiarity facilitates and which in turn enables deeper familiarity with one another's further resources, renews and sustains the spirit of adventure which characterises the best marriages. Of course this fresh strangeness may carry its edge of excitement as suggested above into damaging estrangement. The older resources have to merge with the new in overcoming the dangers and strengthening the communion.

The resources for renewal and development are not, in the Christian vision of reality, merely human. In the Judeo-Christian tradition the ultimate Other encountered in and through the human other is the Holy One of Israel, the transcendent Creator-God and Father of Jesus Christ. In that context marriage was always regarded as a holy state as the bonding of husband and wife reflected the faith bonding with God. In the Hebrew scriptures the relation between God and Israel were depicted in marital terms (Hosea *et al*). The metaphor in the New Testament Letter to Ephesians for marriage is that of the loving union of Christ and his church. In the light of all this, the church formally recognised marriage as a sacrament in the thirteenth century, as an effective sign of the presence and power of God. Self-transcendence to the human other in marriage mirrors and realises faith in the ultimate Transcendent, explicitly for the Christian and perhaps implicitly for others.

There is another stage in all this which has featured from time to time in the Christian tradition. The God of Jesus Christ and that of his followers is of course the Yahweh of Israel and the Abba, Father of Jesus himself. However, the fuller reality of that God becomes apparent through Jesus and the subsequent reflections of his immediate followers. The doctrine of the Triune God, of Father, Son and Holy Spirit, is steadily clarified in the early councils of the church and expressly affirmed in its creeds. It was related to human love relations by various early theologians, some of whom connected the doctrine more immediately to marriage. The distinction, indeed uniqueness and equality, of the three divine persons and their internal loving relationships has been invoked as a model for human community in modern times by theologians like Jürgen Moltmann. That sense of community between unique and equal persons is more clearly characteristic of marriage which already has divine connections. The integration of the Christian couple into the divine Trinity and of the Trinity into the life and love of the couple confirms the depth, exclusivity, fidelity and fruitfulness of marriage. And that fruitfulness, whether it issues in children or not, is by divine power and model enriching the wider world of the whole human community.

CHAPTER SIX

Returning to the God Question

A Note on Patrick Masterson's
'The Sense of Creation: Experience and the God beyond'

A semi-cynical but widely quoted summary of post-Reformation history of religion in Europe went something like this: first to go is the church, then Jesus and finally God. Indeed it was sometimes quoted by Catholics as justification of their survival and expansion in the pre-Vatican II period. Perhaps only the sharpest critics of Vatican II would voice such a summary of the effects of the Council on the Roman Catholic Church itself, although more might be in silent agreement. While moving the central focus from church to Jesus to God might seem (theo)logically appropriate, in Europe over the last few centuries and in Ireland more recently and rapidly it has coincided with, if not directly caused, the current religious crisis, which itself is more and more clearly becoming a crisis of belief-in-God. The apparent signs of such a crisis range from the negative to the positive. Negative signs run from the decline in church attendance and in vocations to the priesthood and religious life, to the increasing neglect of the sacraments such as marriage and baptism or the invocation of them for purely social reasons, to the disappearance of family prayer, to the breakdown of social and sexual morality, and so the litany of woes goes on and on and on. Positively, the secular achievements in science and politics such as respect for personal autonomy and human rights, commitment to the poor at home and development in the third world, campaigns for world peace and against climate change, render a God-given and God-sanctioned morality superfluous. Spiritualities without God and the various worlds of beauty and aesthetics offer further alternatives to the old fashioned religious practices. The passionate reaction by fundamentalist believers, simply anti-secularist or uncritical believers to this disappearance

of religion and faith as they see it, tends to confirm many unbelievers and not a few doubters in the rationality and humanity of
their own position. Of course there is bound to be a large proportion
of uncritical unbelievers, but they are not likely to be persuaded
otherwise by the arguments, whatever about the (loving) actions,
of uncritical believers.

In the context of the Year of Paul, missionary and evangelist, in
the aftermath of the Roman Synod of 'The Word of God in the Life
and Mission of the Church', and with the renewed local and universal interest in the practice of Evangelisation, Christian and
Catholic intellectuals, including philosophers and theologians,
are called in their attempts at scholarly and critical studies to
understand and promote the truth of that mission. This requires a
new kind of engagement with the truth and the truth-tellers, the
love and the love-doers, within and without the boundaries of the
Christian community. Honesty in research, presentation and debate will prevent their work from becoming yet another propaganda exercise to which some styles of apologetics have too often
reduced. Conversation rather than proclamation, dialogue rather
than dictation, living witness in a human family of equals rather
than superior-inferior power-plays are some crucial ways forward for such conversational evangelisation within, between and
beyond the churches.

In reading Patrick Masterson's dense and probing book, it
would be a mistake to adopt it as a kind of pre-evangelisation text
fitting into any official church programme. It is an academic book
by an academic and primarily for academics, and philosophical
academics at that. Yet in the present philosophical and theological
world it is more significant and for a wider range of intelligent
readers than professional Ivory Tower inhabitants. Given the
power and popularity of Dawkins and Hitchens in their anti-God
polemics, Masterson's work is an essential if not so populist anti-
dote. It might be worth remembering the old story about waiting
long and in vain for a bus only to have three come along at the
same time. In this case three superior philosophers have arrived
offering us counter-witness to Dawkins *et al*, namely Masterson,
Canadian Charles Taylor and the former leading atheistic British

philosopher Anthony Flew who recently acknowledged belief in God. The 'Atheists' Bus Campaign' recently initiated in the UK and imitated elsewhere with the slogan 'There probably is no God' is clearly intended to carry the anti-God message. However, its use of the word 'probably' clearly weakens its impact and the consequent advice to people to relax and enjoy themselves might well follow from the contradictory statement that there *is* or probably *is* a God (who creates and thereby loves you).

The prefatory summary affixed to the front of the book indicates the direction and density of Masterson's argument. It may also betoken a warning to the reader, religious, non-religious and anti-religious, of the intellectual and cultural difficulties ahead in an era in which metaphysical analysis and argument are frequently alien. Yet the strenuous efforts of the writer may serve to summon equally strenuous efforts from the reader in response to the superficialities of so much that is written and read on both sides of the religious and philosophical divides.

'Than which greater cannot be conceived'

In settling on a meaning for God, Masterson resorts to that made famous by Anselm in the eleventh century and endorsed by Aquinas two centuries later. So while remaining true to the metaphysical tradition initiated by the Greeks he moves from their idea of a god or gods, who remained part of the cosmos, the world inhabited by human beings, to a concept of the utterly transcendent. That 'greater than which cannot be conceived' is in keeping with the Judeo-Christian and indeed Islamic tradition. Although he does recognise this connection, he is careful to maintain his philosophical independence in distinguishing sharply between meaning and existence, in rejecting Anselm's argument that such a concept of God necessarily involves his existence, the Ontological Argument as it has been known since Kant, and the 'post-Wittgensteinian' stance that attempts by reason to prove the existence of the God of these major religions is both a mistake and unnecessary. Only in the language and practice of such a religion is God's existence established according to these later commentators. With Anselm and Aquinas he also agrees that this 'perfect being' if he exists must exist necessarily, unlike other beings who are all contingent and might or might not exist. Along the same line he argues for a non-mutual real relationship between these contingent beings and the ultimate and perfect being. Contingent beings, creatures, are really related to the ultimate and perfect, their transcendent creator as truly dependent on him but the ulti-mate, the creator is not truly related to them. To be so would mean that he was no longer 'that than which greater cannot be conceived'. He would be modified, added to or subtracted from by creatures.

From the Conditions of Human Experience to Affirming the Existence of God

In the world of Metaphysics, according to Masterson there is no direct argument from human experience affirming the existence of God. Yet that experience provides the ciphers of transcendence as he calls them. By philosophical analysis of such phenomena it is possible to argue indirectly to God's existence. In a series of chap-ters in which he analyses certain human experiences in search of their ultimate justification, he arrives indirectly, as he would claim, at the affirmation of God's existence. In a complex and tech-nical work the two most accessible arguments in the book and the ones on which it is most likely to be generally assessed, are con-tained in Chapter 5. 'Knowledge and Transcendence' and Chapter 6, 'Morality and Transcendence'. Chapter 7, 'Co-Existence and Transcendence', is an interesting re-working of Aquinas's Fourth Argument. Chapter 9 deals mainly with the work of Irish philosopher Richard Kearney in his volume *The God Who Maybe*. So there is much to chew on and the non-professional philosopher at least may have some real difficulties in digesting.

That non-professional may find Chapter 5 on 'Knowledge and Transcendence' the most accessible and digestible. In search of a reasonable interpretation of the human capacity to understand the world in ordinary living as well as in the various scientific modes, Masterson asks how human intelligence and the intelligi-bility of the world form such a purposeful fit. Rejecting the intel-lectual evasion of people like Bertrand Russell that that's just the way things are, and the inadequate biological attempt to reduce human thought and subjectivity to biology, Masterson finds the only satisfying solution in the existence of an external free Creator. The argument may not be reduced to a form of creationism and is not a competitor in the science classroom because it is a strictly philosophical and metaphysical argument. To invoke a distinction he makes later in the book, and which applies to all the arguments advanced here, an argument may be cogent while not convincing to all reasonable people of good will, as for example already convinced atheists. Conversely of course an argument may be convincing without being cogent, as the worlds of advertising and propaganda should constantly remind us. A further illuminating aspect of the treatment of human knowledge here is the asymmetry of the relationship between the knower and the known which the author emphasises. While the relationship of the subject-knower to the object known is real, the relation of the object known to the knower is only logical. In other words, the knower is really dependent on and changed by the object known, the object is independent of and unchanged by the knower. This corresponds for Masterson to the asymmetrical relationship between Creator and creature in the major religions, where creatures are utterly dependent and affected by the Creator while the Creator is utterly independent of and unaffected by them. This theme pervades all the other arguments advanced in the course of the book,

f Chapter 5 is the most accessible, as I believe it is, it is obviously so tightly argued and sometimes so technically expressed that it remains a difficult read, but the reader with a serious interest in philosophical and religious issues should not be discouraged from tackling such a rich piece of analysis. A more engaging argument, for this reader at least, is offered in Chapter 6 on 'Morality and Transcendence'. Indeed for many people it may be the most attractive, even convincing, argument for God's existence. Masterson provides a fair account of Kant's argument from morality to the affirmation of God, but his predominant interest is in the moral philosophy of twentieth century philosopher Emmanuel Levinas and in his major work, *Totality and Infinity*.

Accepting, at least for the sake of this argument, Levinas' view

of the philosophical indeed metaphysical priority of ethics over
ontology, Masterson focuses on the self and Other relationship as
the central ethical and so metaphysical reality. It is face to face
with the unique and irreducible Other (person) that the self dis-
covers ethical obligation and motivation. Because in the Levinas
vision the Other dominates the encounter, the self cannot make
equal and reciprocal claims. The relationship is once again asymmetrical. Human beings taken together cannot form a closed or
comprehensive totality; infinity is the apt word for the range of
such irreducible beings in their asymmetrical relationships and
only a power external to them can provide the fraternity they
need and experience. This is the power of the creator who creates
out of nothing, excluding the emanation from divinity itself or the
transformation of some simply pre-existing primordial material.
Both of the latter theories would be unable to account for the irreducibility of the human being or for the consequent justice implications of encounter with the Other. Its primary moral and justice
demand is: 'Thou shalt not murder'. Such emanations or transform-
ations would turn the human 'collectivity' into a deterministic
totality with totalitarian undertones. Creation out of nothing confirms the irreducibility in the asymmetrical relationship between
Creator and creatures as already evidenced in the relationship between human creatures themselves in their primary moral relationship. The transcendence of the Other to the self is ultimately
grounded in the transcendence of Creator to creature which also
permits the true fraternity of 'infinity'. While this crude summary
is far from adequate to the original argument of Levinas or its
effective development by Masterson, it may lead the interested
reader to serious reflection on what I believe to be the most persuasive argument in the book for the affirmation of God's existence. Some further influences of Levinas may be found in this volume in the chapters on marriage and preaching and more immediately related to morality in earlier volumes over the decades.

    Masterson's treatment of Aquinas' fourth argument in chapter
7, entitled 'Analogy and Transcendence', offers a serious rethink
of the more usual interpretation or still more usual dismissal of
this fourth argument. However, although to be highly recom-

mended to students of Aquinas and of the philosophy of religion generally, it is too complex for the brief treatment possible here. As with the other arguments but even more effectively, it recovers both the value of Aquinas' pioneering work and the continuing validity of philosophical reasoning in relation to God's existence and nature. For theologians, perhaps such philosophising suggests a move from the often superficial introduction to theology of the old seminary courses to the development and deepening of theology and theologians in dialogue with the great philosophers, historical and contemporary.

Masterson's profound if short work bears re-reading and re-meditating. He inevitably leaves some important questions unresolved. His acceptance of Levinas' priority of ethics over ontology will disturb philosophers of his own broad school and is not obviously consistent with his metaphysical argument in relation to knowledge and transcendence or on the analogy of being. How far all such metaphysical analysis is culturally conditioned by a certain Western tradition from the Greeks through the medievals to the twentieth century might deserve fuller examination. His overall treatment of science and philosophy seems sound if brief, although biologists might look for more attention to their positions and sub-atomic physicists might take issue with the view that the object known is never affected by the knowing subject. Masterson, on the evidence available, could effectively meet any such objections. How he will deal with the relations between Creator and creatures in the context of Christian faith may be more interesting for Christians. Can his presentation of the asymmetrical relationship do justice to a God of love involved in covenant relations with his people to the point of becoming one of them ? His treatment of all these difficulties, when it comes, will make for even more rewarding reading.

Conclusion
'Anselm and Aquinas developed a philosophical understanding of "Creation" as an asymmetrical relationship between the world and God, that is, that the world is finally related to God in a relationship of total dependence, but God is in no way related to or

modified by this created world. This idea of an asymmetrical relationship is the key concept unifying all aspects of this book which
discusses three main inter-related questions in a philosophical
discussion about God – the question of meaning, the question of
existence, the question of co-existence.'

This summary quoted at the start of his work makes clear that
Masterson's return to metaphysics is not for the intellectually
faint-hearted or light-headed. His recovery of the metaphysical
arguments about the meaning, existence and co-existence of God
will offer intellectual comfort and substance to many believers
who have been fobbed off with easy and misleading versions of
natural theology, provided they can stay the course, master the
language and cope with the technical acuity of it all. No doubt
some will survive and enjoy the crackling philosophical joust.
Others of Christians faith may look forward to Professor
Masterson's follow-up volume when he will attempt to translate
the meaning of God in Trinitarian terms and the asymmetrical relationship between God and humanity into the language of
incarnation and redemption, resurrection and providence. Even
before that he may resort, as he hints, to arguments from imagination and beauty, rather than simply reason, to buttress his move
from the empirical to the transcendent, a noble enterprise he has
so effectively undertaken in the present volume.

CHAPTER SEVEN

The Word of God

The human words we must use; the human words God / scriptures must use and their ambiguities; new wine in old wineskins and while 'the old is good' (Lk 5), it often requires an educated taste or the gift of discernment.

Many words used in preaching, teaching and various verbal proclamations of the word of God may by sheer repetition claim the mantle of orthodoxy, but unless they are renewed by the Spirit of God, supplemented by fresh, contemporary and faithful human words and witnessed by the lives of the proclaimers, they get drowned in the political, cultural cacophony surrounding them. The 'ears to hear' are too frequently deaf to the Word of God because of the sheer noise and banality of the immediate wordscape.

One cleanser of the littered wordscape in world or in church is undoubtedly silence. But it must be a rich and so a nurtured silence. Such nurturing may occur in various ways through profound human experiences – experiences that are personal as in love or bereavement; social as in family, local, national achievement or disaster; cultural as in listening to great music, reading a great poem or novel, watching a great drama on stage or screen; and of course natural in the presence of ocean, mountain or sunset.

These are the silences we may take with us into church and prayer, as Jesus did when he went up into the mountains to pray or crossed the lake to get away from the crowds. The silences brought on by these human experiences are a form of *praeparatio evangelica* in giving us the taste and the skills for the deeper experiences of listening to the Word in prayerful attention. They may also lead us into the mysterious silence of God's own presence as gateways through the worldly to the transcendent, through creation to the Creator self.

Silence, creative, critical and receptive, as both preparation and foundation for the proclamation and reception of God's word is essential but never enough. Otherwise why should God have bothered with human language at all, with *dabhar* in the Hebrew dispensation and *logos* become *sarx* in the Christian dispensation and all the other sounds and sights of creation and new creation? Out of the silence and in the power of the divine *dabhar* and divine *logos* we are called to discern the subtle soundings and delicate lightings of the gospel which the contemporary human achievements, ambiguities and confusions always embody.

The generators of creative silence, partially listed above, are also bearers of the creative mark of God, however opaquely at times. Such an unlikely theatrical example as Samuel Beckett's *Waiting for Godot* may prove for many theatre-goers a cleansing experience to the point where the banalities and superstitions of some conventional beliefs and believers are dissolved – verbal and physical play of Didi and Gogo; the master-slave interlude of Pozzo and Lucky; the message of deferral by the 'innocent' boy – all act as counterpoint to the despairing wait with its under- and over-tones of a world about Calvary with its dashed expectation of resurrection. In many ways that is our world. Yet without the despair would we be ready for the promise and reality of resurrection? Without the promise purged of easy escapism by the despair of Calvary would we continue to believe as we wait?

Most theatre-goers leave in sombre silence after the performance. It may for many be a generative silence, generative of a fresh hope and faith.

There are simpler, clearer and more direct human experiences which may have similar cleansing effects in preparing us to proclaim and to hear anew the transforming word of God. It goes without saying that the proclaimer must be transformed by the word he proclaims, if he is to assist in the effective transforming of the listener.

Not all cultural or worldly contexts are of suffering and despair. The story of Cana should be a reminder of that. Celebration in its human joy and creativity, at birth and baptism for example, is more deeply generative and revealing of divine and human reality.

Celebration and lamentation are major characteristics of human culture, and of the human condition and appear as such in the biblical traditions. The active ministry of Jesus might be summarised as one of hospitality (including the excluded, eating and drinking with sinners) and of healing (spiritual, psychological and physical). It is in the context of that active ministry he spoke as one having authority over the word of God, unlike his opponents, the scribes and Pharisees. It is in that active ministry of hospitality and healing, which so frequently belong together, that his disciples, the church, may hope to proclaim effectively his word as God's word. In attempting to illustrate that, we will look at how the word may be discovered and proclaimed through hospitality and healing in three dimensions of the contemporary engagement of church and world, the intellectual, the social, and the ecumenical.

Intellectual Hospitality and Healing
In his sometimes controversial Regensburg address of 2006 Pope Benedict dwelt on the necessary and valuable dialogue between Christian faith and human reason. Allowing for the western cultural limitations which sometimes attend such claims, the honest, creative-critical and persistent conversation between the Hebrew-Christian scriptures and the contemporary secular sciences, and within the scriptures themselves, is an essential part of the word of God itself in its Creation and New Creation modes. It would be wildly exaggerating to say that a spirit of intellectual hospitality and healing characterises much of such dialogue in Western countries today.

Fundamentalism is the most potent enemy of such hospitable and healing intellectual exchange and it affects believers and unbelievers alike, from Pat Buchanan of the Christian Right in the USA to Richard Dawkins, biologist in Oxford University.

Intellectual hospitality is not intellectual surrender anymore than intellectual healing is some kind of conversion. Yet there is a listening, and receiving, a reflecting and possible revisioning by both sides, which can be enriching for them and for the whole intellectual and indeed human community.

Called and empowered by the word of God, Christians have to take the first and the continuing if often frustrating steps in promoting this dialogue. This will exclude angry dismissals of opponents as it will include admissions of past and present Christian failure in love and truth and justice. Above all it will require serious attempts to understand the others' difficulties, however bizarre they may at times appear. It will involve an effort to learn from these opposing positions. Finally of course, it will seek in the light of these debates to expose as clearly and accurately as possible and in a spirit of love the Christian position in the controverted area. Such intellectual hospitality and healing have led to the true development of doctrine on which John Henry Newman reflected so fruitfully and which still challenges the church.

Orthodoxy in teaching is always there to be defended intellectually and in reconciliation or healing. But it is also there to be expanded in the same spirit.

Social Hospitality and Healing

In Ireland today, in Europe and in the wider world we are moving from a time of intense internal division between long time neighbours who are or are becoming coexisting, even co-operating, citizens. Northern Ireland is one of the more obvious and, it is to be hoped, successful examples of such transition. Social hospitality and healing is urgently needed to overcome the bitter hostility and hurt, which range from the family and locality to the gender and ethnic, the national and international. The recent Oxfam Report (*The Guardian*, 11 October 2007) reveals that wars in Africa since the end of the Cold War have cost as much financially as international aid to the same continent in the same period, without counting the cost in human lives to combatants and to civilians, still more, and mainly of women and children.

In the thunder of such violence and war, the word of God will get a poor hearing without the preparatory work of God's reconciliation, the task of those whom Paul describes as 'Ambassodors of Reconciliation', the followers of the Christ in whom God was reconciling the world with himself (2 Cor 5). In its commitment to such reconciliation and to the eventual elimination of war as the last of the great human barbarisms, the church may be doing its most important work in creating a context in which the word of God, the word of God's peace be with you may be fruitfully heard.

Ecumenical Hospitality and Healing

The tragedy of war and human violence has a long history of religious and indeed Christian complicitly. The bitterness of religious divisions has resulted in some of the world's most destructive conflicts with little room for the healing and reconciling divine word. That complicity is still around. There is, however, a more serious attempt to show hospitality to those of other Christian and religious traditions and regular if limited healing rites and exercises between the religiously separated. Yet it all seems so little and so late in face of the historic depth of the divisions and the continuing scandal to unbelievers. Hospitality and healing between Christians must be intensified way beyond the present tepid efforts if further serious inter-religious dialogue is to be successful and if the hospitable and healing word of God is to have a wider audience.

That should include for separated Christians who are yet united by baptism in the one body of Christ, and seek to follow his example, shared social service of the needy, common religious study in school, seminary and university, more frequent prayer services and retreats together and, with due preparation, at least the occasional mutual hospitality of Jesus' own memorial sacrament of the Eucharist.

Through such ecumenical gatherings, the word of God will not only reach the immediate participants but also the wider hungry sheep who will be looking on and hoping to be fed.

PART II: NEW DREAMS

CHAPTER EIGHT

The Good News in Moral Theology: Of Hospitality, Healing and Hope

Celebrating Kevin Kelly

When Kevin Kelly began to study and then to teach moral theology it was not notable for its good news. Professional moral theologians and the textbooks of that era were not what is termed in other contexts 'gospel-greedy'. Indeed Jesus and his joyous message of the imminent reign of God were scarcely mentioned. The 'bad news' of sin, in number and kind, predominated. In the subsequent transformation of moral theology and its rediscovery of Jesus's good news, Kevin Kelly has played a very significant role. For students and colleagues, lay and clerical, Kevin has himself become 'good news', but not without paying a price exacted by those whom Pope John XXIII dubbed, at the beginning of Vatican II, 'the prophets of doom'.

Without attempting any serious evaluation of either the developments in moral theology over the last half-century or of Kevin's splendid contribution to them, this essay seeks to elaborate some aspects of the good news implied, if seldom made explicit, in these developments. Given some previous efforts to address similar issues and a certain weakness for alliteration, it did not surprise me to find these aspects listed in my mind as 'Hospitality, Healing and Hope', although in some other contexts the order might be different.

OF HOSPITALITY IN MORAL THEOLOGY

Beyond the Inhospitable Discipline and its God
Whatever about male human origins according to popular lore, morality, in its Hebrew, Greek and even Christian forms and in various combinations of these, too often seemed to be from Mars; too often a cold military style code of behaviour demanding total obedience and lacking any concessions to the varieties and vag-

aries of real human beings. That form and style inevitably suggested a warrior, punitive, even vindictive God, certainly not the
Hebrew God of loving kindness (*hesed*) or the God who is love
(*agape*), the Abba-Father God of Jesus and the New Testament.
Out of that distortion of Jewish-Christian morality and of its God
grew the inhospitable discipline known as moral theology or, in
this last half-century, more correctly as manual moral theology.
Not that we should or can dismiss the justice and judging dimensions of the God and morality of Israel and of Jesus but that we
must integrate them, nay, subordinate them to the two great commandments of love of God and love of neighbour and their divine
author. Justice continues to give love its cutting edge without de-
humanising or de-divinising that love. It is in such a theological
framework that hospitality as characteristic/virtue of the creating, saving and sanctifying God, and of the human creature as
image, child and temple of the same God, may raise its lovely
head.

The Garden Party of Creation and its Divine Host/Artist
Although there are numerous examples of the practice and value
of hospitality in both the Hebrew and Christian scriptures, from
the father of Hebrew and Christian faith, Abraham, to the centre
of Christian faith, Jesus, and to these scriptures we shall return.
The heart of divine hospitality and the source of its human counterpart lie in the originating and continuing divine act of creation,
continuing in the face of persistent human refusal of that divine
graciousness. In face of that human refusal called sin, the inexhaustible divine hospitality emerges as New Creation in Jesus. To
appreciate the depth and range of the human call to hospitality, its
centrality to Christian life and to the examined Christian life in
moral theology, it is necessary to begin at the beginning, with the
God who created the heavens and the earth, saw that they were
good and invited man and woman created in the divine image to
share, enjoy and care for them.

   The Genesis accounts of Creation combine some of the features
of a celebratory Garden Party given by a generous host with those
of an Art Exhibition in which the artist also displays the earlier

stages of his now completed work. The host-artist is of course the Creator-God. And the artworks of Creation as well as the celebratory food and drink are available as free gifts for the enjoyment of all the guests, in this context all generations of the human race. Jahweh, the God of Israel, appears as generous host and creative artist right through the history of Israel, as that history is recorded, prophetically judged and anticipated, celebrated and lamented in the Hebrew scriptures.

The divine host-creator sets the tone as he recognises the good and celebrates the goods of his creation-party offerings and welcomes the first human guests as reflections of his own goodness and encourages them both to enjoy and care for what has been provided. Even at this first mythological but truth-bearing party, when the host's back is turned the guests are tempted to get above themselves and to misbehave. It is ever so but this host, at first offended, reaches more deeply into his resources of creative hospitality and loving kindness to maintain divine-human friendship in forgiveness, renewal of promise and celebration. East of Eden, in this land of Cain in which all human beings still partially reside with all their tragic failures and scandals, the role of divine host and the rule of divine hospitality persist. At their best the human guests recognise the role and accept the rule to the point of employing role and rule to act as hosts and guests of one another. As carers and sharers of the offerings of the divine creation they behave in what prophets from Isaiah to Jesus might call a just and loving way.

In its more conventional and restricted sense, the language and practice of hospitality recur in biblical narrative and prophetic injunction. Abraham's reception of the strangers in Genesis 18 is the more notable example. The inhospitality of others, such as the people of Sodom, prepares the way for the condemnations by Amos and his prophetic colleagues of the neglect of the needy, the poor, the widow, the orphan and the stranger. Strangers as the Israelites were in Egypt, and beneficiaries as they were in their hunger and thirst in their Exodus in the desert through the generosity of their God with manna from the heavens and water from the rock, they are called to show similar hospitality to the neighbour and visitor in need. The Messianic land and age of promise, flowing with milk and honey, will typify the fullness of divine and human hospitality.

That fullness filters ambiguously through the nativity stories in the gospels of Luke and Mark. The re-creative generosity of God in sending his own Son meets with the hospitable responses of Mary and Joseph, of Zachariah and Elizabeth, of the angels and the shepherds, of the wise men from the east, of Simeon and Anna, but suffers the rejection of the innkeeper and the murderous hostility of Herod, all this in parallel to the glory and the tragedy of Genesis. In the more nearly biographical sections of all four gospels, the hospitality of God in Jesus, particularly towards the poor and excluded, and the return of hospitality by these to Jesus, are key to understanding the new divine-human relationship already in being and yet to be completed.

This active table-fellowship hospitality finds vivid expression in Jesus' teaching through parable and exhortation. In John, the most abstract of the evangelists in so many ways, Jesus' active ministry opens and closes with a party, the wedding party at Cana and the farewell party in the Upper Room in Jerusalem. It is unnecessary and would be tedious for gospel readers to rehearse all the events from the feeding of the five thousand to the parables of Luke to the final judgement account in Matthew to be aware of how deeply hospitality enters into the ministry and teaching of Jesus and how it is still invoked in the post-resurrection stories. With all that taken for granted one may move on to how hospitality relates to the accepted major characteristics of Christian living and so shapes that living, to how it may provide the basic guidance for that living which moral theology also aspires to describe and prescribe.

Hospitality and Justice
Although charity/love played a pivotal role in the recent renewal of moral theology, justice in various forms may be more relevant here; partly because theological discussion of it too has developed in remarkable ways over the last decades and partly because at first inspection anyway it may prove more challenging than charity

to any central position for hospitality in moral theology. The harder edges of justice in morality, law and theology with their retributive, retaliative and punitive echoes seem far removed from the generous and forgiving spirit of hospitality. *Fiat justitia, ruat coelum* may be of secular rather than religious origin but few religious traditions have escaped its influence and that influence operated sometimes at least to organised religion's benefit. The injustices practised within the Christian tradition for example, even against its own believers including theologians, were not often overcome by the church's formal adherence to the two great commandments. Such injustices were and are violations of hospitality, of the openness to the other involved in giving each person her due.

There is clearly a danger here that the violation of any moral virtue or moral commandment may be re-described as a violation of hospitality without any additional light being shed on the moral reality at issue. In the case of justice it might be argued that hospitality is a broader and richer moral category which restores justice to its proper place as a quality of interpersonal relations and not simply a duty to be done. In such a context, for example, the preference for the poor so wonderfully illustrated in the parable of the feast in Luke 13, would enjoy both the hard edge of justice and the *sans frontiers* thrust of the biblical and divine outreach. In a different fashion, the controlling value and virtue of hospitality would at once endorse the protection of society's vulnerable through the legal and court system, while replacing the punitive and vindictive dimension of that system with a serious attempt at restorative justice for the offended party, at real rehabilitation for the offender and at mutual reconciliation in the society itself. Very little of these dimensions is evident in our present legal, court and prison systems. The messianic promise of liberation to prisoners in Isaiah and Luke 4, as well as the Jesus' self-identification with the prisoner you came to visit in Matthew 25, call for such hospitality-justice and not in the satirical sense of regular usage with prisoners described as guests of Her Majesty.

A more obvious central role for hospitality may be found in the whole area of medical ethics. How far it would provide fresh insight into the usual boundary cases including abortion, IVF, embryonic stem-cell research, drug experimentation and assisted suicide would be open to question by certain proponents of these practices. It would at least provide a richer human context for their discussion than that of the purely autonomous, unrelated, individual human being. It should also deepen the motivation and commitment of all those engaged in both medical care and research. The origins of the medical hospital and the more recent development of hospice and hospice care for the dying are eloquent testimony to the role of hospitality in the service of the sick. Beyond this, a hospitable society would be more aware of its obligations to all its sick and pressurise its government to provide fair and adequate care for all.

One last and very difficult example is that of international relations. For most statesmen and commentators the first and often the only realistic demand is to look after the national interest. A collective egoism predominates and is defended as the primary duty of leaders whose responsibility is to the their own people, whether or not they elected them. It has become increasingly difficult to confine or define the national interest of any particular state, however powerful it may appear by the usual criteria of military and economic strength. So the international interest has almost always to be considered. Unilateralism and exceptionalism even by the very powerful appear increasingly self-defeating. However, to identify the international interest with that of a coalition of the willing and powerful, as seems the present trend, may be successful in the shorter and more limited terms of real politik but it can never be entirely stable and enduring. More significantly in moral terms, it is deeply oppressive of the poorer and weaker nations. It is profoundly inhospitable to so many of its own kind, other human beings. Only when international relations and international law are rooted in a universal hospitality for the stranger, the poor, the weak and the sojourner, to invoke biblical categories, will the there be a real prospect of a genuine united nations and of a just and peaceful world.

Other difficult domains of moral discourse and practice would, I believe, benefit from re-integration into the hospitable range of the creating and redeeming God, and of the created and redeemed human community. Sexuality may be one of the more difficult domains, as it is in every moral vision. Saving the earth should be one of the easier ones given Creator-God as host, humans as the pre-eminent guests of Creator and creation, hosts as well as guests of one another and of the rest of creation. And all this founded in the engagement of the Triune God, whose reign is at hand but not complete.

OF HEALING

The hospitality stories and their moral insights from Eden to Emmaus have their limitations as they also reveal the failures of their human protagonists. Divine hospitality in creation and salvation is destined to be a healing hospitality as well. The messianic promises, their fulfilment in the life and ministry of Jesus and their earlier partial anticipation in the history of Israel, focus on that healing hospitality. However pure the divine or even human invitation and welcome may be as they face their guests, in establishing and developing personal, social or political relationships, human weaknesses, flaws and failures are endemic. We humans are sinners all not only in relation to God but in relation to one another. The good news moral theology, however, includes the healing in the hospitality as so many of Jesus' actions and parables demonstrate. 'Which is it easier to say, "Thy sins are forgiven thee" or "Take up thy bed and walk"?' (Mk :2:9).

In elaborating a Christian moral vision and any moral code derived from it, healing and forgiveness must be intrinsic to it. An idealistic moral system based on virtue (Aristotle), duty (Kant) or law (Decalogue/Manuals) is not adequate to the human condition and its relationships because the healing and forgiveness are extrinsic and come after the fact, the fact of the inherently limited human condition as physically and morally vulnerable, as sinful and mortal. And despite the perduring goodness of Creator and Creation and crucial healing accomplished in Jesus Christ, the holistic healing of the divine hospitality is yet to be. The historical earnest (*arrabon*), of which Paul speaks in his Second Letter to the Corinthians and which we already enjoy, reaches its fulfilment only in the eschaton. The interaction between hospitality and healing in all moral understanding and moral endeavour underlines the eschatological dimension of moral theology which is in itself always flawed and incomplete, always in search of the fuller truth and practice, indeed the fuller truth through practice, including mistaken practice. That fuller, more healed moral truth and practice reflect the moral progress of the past in the exclusion of slavery, torture and capital punishment for example, in the restrictions on warfare through the developing criteria for just war over the past centuries and the possibility of a total moral ban on war in the century(ies) ahead. In all these, better moral understanding and practice have benefited from the interaction of hospitality and healing. In the case of slavery, for example, where, as in the nineteenth century, simple liberation could not satisfy the demands of hospitality, so grievously violated by the system, without healing of both master and slave and of the destructive impact of the system. Such healing and hospitality are far from complete in social terms, while new forms of the old oppression continue to surface.

In other moral areas, practice and understanding worthy of hospitality are not attainable without a great deal of healing. Sexuality provides many and difficult examples of this. Sexual development of young people depends on the hospitable care, support and understanding of adults, parents and mentors, who are often far from being open and integrated, healed and mature guides and companions in their own sexual lives. More progress could be made in morally good sexual understanding and practice if the hospitality, which must always include justice and respect for the other, were offered in a healing way by somebody aware of his own continuing need of healing. As in other moral relationships, the creative interaction between hospitality, the loving welcome of the other, and healing care are essential to the followers of him who spent so much time with prostitutes and sinners. The insights of the moral theology of sexuality into masturbation, homosexuality and contraception, to take a few recently controverted examples, will continue to develop effectively only in such a hospitable and healing context, with all the intellectual, emotional and practical implications which that involves.

HOPE

The final H-word in this brief excursus into Christian moral theology is the final historical H-word, indeed the final word of all Christian theology, Hope. In the human understanding and practice of the Christian moral life the limitations of creatureliness and failure are endemic. As Paul expresses it, we are saved in hope – we see now through a glass darkly, and so the call to perfection of mind and morality remains out of reach. Not that we are not called to seek perfection and do not have some real grasp of moral truth. But the fullness is beyond us. The eschatological dimension of our very being is at once the source of our frustration and the basis of our striving. In affecting to teach the world and to bear witness to the life and love of God in Jesus, Christians are necessarily dependent on the Spirit who will finally lead them into all truth. But it will be *finally*, so that their present moral understanding and practice is subject to that eschatological restraint as they attempt to follow the Spirit in the Hope that protects from the arrogance and presumption of certain absolutist positions and from the despair and disintegration of certain relativist positions.

Even with this summary account of hospitality, healing and hope as integral to a theology of the Christian life or moral theology, the good news of moral theology to which Kevin so effectively witnessed may be clarified a little further.

CHAPTER NINE

The Kenosis of Preaching

'Have this mind among yourselves, which is yours in Christ Jesus, who though he was in the form of God, did not account equality to God a thing to be grasped, but emptied himself ('alla 'eauton 'ekenosen, Gk), taking the form of a servant, being born in the likeness of men. And being found in human form he humbled himself and became obedient unto death, even death on a cross.' (Phil 2:5-8)

There can hardly be a more inspiring call to preachers than that of St Paul to the people of Philippi. Translating this call into the more explicit instructions for the modern preacher must always, in its very verbal expansion, be a form of reduction. The inspiring and compact imagery of poetry is diminished in the prose of explanation. Books or articles of instruction, frequently helpful, may do more harm than good. At the levels of religion, ethics, poetry and art and other higher human activities, they are seldom of benefit beyond novitiate or apprenticeship. It may be that some practitioners never get past the novice or apprentice stage. Better then perhaps to abandon the practice for some other more adapted to one's gifts. Not every imaginative person is called or suited to be a particular kind of artist or even to being an artist at all, and may more quickly discover their real gifts by leaving aside their present book(s) of instruction. Similarly not every ordained priest is suited to preaching, however carefully trained and however many books of instruction or of sermon aids he studies.

However, in the actual situation of today's church (it was not always so and may not be so again), every priest must in his own best way announce the gospel of Jesus Christ. For all priests that best way is first of all having the mind and living the life of Christ as Paul insists. Beyond that they will try to put into their own words the meaning of this Christ-mind and Christ-life, however inadequate their minds, lives and words may be. The first lesson on these preaching-words emerges from familiarity with the imaginative, poetic and narrative strength of the great passages in scripture, as already illustrated from Paul.

Locating the preacher in regard to a particular homily or sermon is a first requirement. It is in that precise location that he is to take the form of the servant of the word after the manner of Christ. Following through that location enables the preacher and his/her instructor to chart the ways and levels of self-emptying (*kenosis*) called for in the preparation and delivery of the particular homily. The location has many dimensions to it, including the location of the preacher in his own spiritual, pastoral, intellectual and even physical location, such as age and health. Elsewhere I deal with some of these dimensions more personal to the priest-preacher. Here my concern is with the location immediately confronting him.

There is the immediate occasion, a regular Sunday or daily Mass, a major liturgical feast, a special occasion like a wedding, a funeral or other parochial or family celebration. This demands the first self-emptying or surrender by the preacher to the actual liturgical occasion and will differ from each Sunday in Ordinary Time to Pentecost Sunday and from funeral to wedding. Such surrender requires prayerful preparation although experience will facilitate that, certainly for frequently recurring occasions such as regular Sundays. For Good Friday or Christmas Day the preacher will need to start afresh for his own sake as well as that of his congregation. Each of these two feasts illustrate deep dimensions of what Paul calls the *kenosis* of Christ and it is to these deep and differing dimensions that the preacher must attend, to the point of being taken over by them, to the point of surrender. The Christmas *kenosis* manifests the first of the great mysteries as the Author of Creation emerges as a helpless creature from his mother's womb in some poor peasant's stable. The symbolic rather than the literal sense of Luke's account is what should concern us here as we try to prepare ourselves to announce this paradoxically good news to church and world. We might well have spent time preparing and training for this. Although each Advent Sunday had its own demands, the cumulative effect of the season would reach its climax on this day for the conscientious and by now celebratory preacher. Good Friday has another kenotic tale to tell. And for all the six weeks of the Lenten preparation, few preachers are ready for the despair and disbelief which that day could provoke. Such steadfast attention to the highs and lows of the liturgical year are stressful and yet stretching for the seriously committed Christian preacher. And there will be the inevitable, sometimes serious lapses by the preacher who is still an actual sinner if would-be saint.

Surrender to the scriptures of the day is an obvious demand for an authentic homily. Some of these readings are prescribed or selected as appropriate to the occasion, be it Easter Day or Wedding Day. So preparation for the particular liturgy, remote and immediate, already includes their inhabiting one's mind and heart. Yet their broader biblical and theological contexts in the Old and New Testaments, as well as in the later tradition, should form the implicit if unspoken background out of which the congregation on this particular occasion is addressed. As both Easter and Wedding celebrations are primarily celebrations of new life, they might carry biblical echoes of other great celebrations from Creation to Exodus, from Bethlehem to Cana to Emmaus, from Isaiah's depiction of the banquet which the Lord is preparing for his people to Ezechiel's vision of the Valley of the Dry Bones, to the new heavens and the new earth promised in the Book of Revelation. For weddings in particular, the innumerable biblical variations on the themes of divine and human love should, if not explicitly expressed in the readings chosen, be close to the surface of the homilist's thought and word. In the actual homily, the richness of the unspoken background may be more influential than the readings or more explicit citations from the scriptures.

Influential with whom? With the particular congregation assembled about the preacher first of all, and perhaps less directly with their families and friends. (Some people still speak of good and bad sermons they have recently heard.) The liturgical occasion with its scriptural readings leads to the more profound and mysterious *kenosis* of the preacher before the preached to, the actual congregation on the day. For that to happen he must know them, not all or perhaps any of them personally, although knowing some of them should be the norm. But he must know them in their general background and common humanity, in their gender, ethnic, cultural, economic, professional and age diversity, in their shared joys and griefs, hopes and fears. Much of this may be gleaned from his previous encounters with similar people as well as from the stories of his own life and that of his family and friends. Yet he must consider each congregation anew, even his regular Sunday congregation, which he only gradually gets to know well and which in any case is always changing however slightly in its composition and in individual lives. It is into these lives that he must empty himself and his faith, hope and love in words prompted, perhaps even inspired, by the liturgical occasion and its scriptures. Such self-emptying may have its shadowside for the assembly through his weaknesses or theirs, but it will avoid mastering the congregation in any exhibitionist or prideful way. Mastery is not the role of the Christian preacher but that of humble service.

The service of self-emptying as rendered by the preacher is fuelled by his sense of the occasion and his surrender to the readings in their particulars and in their larger contexts. But the focus of his service is the people whom he is addressing. The Jewish philosopher Emmanuel Levinas regards the presence of the Other(s) as enabling responsibility in a response he describes as *kenosis*, establishing an asymmetrical or non-mutual relationship between self and Other(s). It is the others which release the self into its true self as the self-for, and the asymmetry precludes the expectation or reception of any direct response from the Other(s). Whatever the further application of this insight it seems that in the Christian situation of preaching it is helpful, provided the preacher approaches it as he should in the Pauline spirit of the *kenosis* of Christ. Genuine encounter with the others of the congregation, surrender to them, offers the preacher liberation into his true self. It is an occasion of grace and salvation. The presence of the others in this liturgical situation becomes a mediation of divine presence and divine grace, or divine trace as Levinas might also want to say. The Other(s) of the congregation are saviours, relating closely Word and Sacrament as the Christian tradition affirms.

Before pursuing further the human and divine dimensions of the Others as congregation, the content and style of the preaching itself need to be examined, not least because the preacher's liberation by his audience may be influenced by that content and style. The closer the preaching hews in content to the central mysteries of the faith and their ethical implications, the more the liberating/saving effect of the audience is likely to be effective. Only a seriously Christian content can expect to mediate the self-giving which in context becomes Christian *kenosis* and salvation. Such content is not sufficient of itself to reach the audience and set the preacher free. There are probably many more sermons heavy with 'theology' which effect no such *kenosis* than there are those so content-light that they could not embody any *kenosis*. Given the appropriate content as suggested by occasion, readings and congregation, the self-emptying comes down to personal authenticity as expressed in composition and delivery.

Authenticity may not be taken for granted. It is obviously violated in just reading out or borrowing heavily from somebody else's work. Given the interdependence of the historic Christian community already alluded to in various ways, every preacher draws on the wisdom and the words of others. However, what he speaks and how he speaks must be of himself. The words, images and ideas inspired by others must have become not just memorised or even intellectually internalised. They need to be painfully absorbed, suffered through and transformed in the crucible of his own life. What emerges from this experience will undoubtedly be his own but that will come to completion in the actual delivery. He must speak with his own voice as well as in his own words.

Those will be the voice and words of saint and sinner. Pious disguise pre-empts true encounter with the Others. It is the actual sinner and would-be-saint who empties himself before the congregation and is rewarded, without any demand for return, by their real presence in saving grace. Not only is he honest to his life-experience but by continuously calling on his however limited imagination and literary experience he finds the right words and images in which to express that experience. The style is the man in this *kenotic* exercise of preaching.

In Christian understanding this style is not only the man. It is the God-man, the Word made flesh, human flesh, in order that human flesh be divinised, or more accurately reveal its potential for transformation through encounter with the divine. The preacher cannot control or even simulate this. As the congregation encountered liberates/transforms in grace the preacher, it does so in virtue of the enabling God en-fleshed among them. The initiative is always with God in asymmetrical terms. The authentic preacher is no achiever of himself and he is not in some mutual saving(s) economy. The congregation is likewise not the author of the preacher's or its own transformation. The Other beyond the others, and in turn vivifying them, is however obscurely the God of Paul's *kenosis*, the Absolute Other whose presence is sensed, even recognised in the preaching encounter. In a more familiar and accessible idiom, Levinas described the encounter with the many in terms of justice. This comes close to the thought of Aquinas. For him, justice was of course the correct relationship with the other(s). And religion was an aspect of justice as directed to the Absolute Other, God.

CHAPTER TEN

Reading Thomas Kinsella

Peppercanister 26 and 27
An avid reader of poetry, I am a reluctant commentator. This is
partly out of the conviction that poetry should be allowed to speak
for itself and not cluttered with prose and prosaic comment. It is
perhaps born still more of fear, fear of the mystery of the particular
poem and fear of the personal inadequacy of the non-poet, not unrelated to the fears of the theologian in face of deeper mysteries,
divine, cosmic and human, scriptural and sacramental. But the delight provided by the poet and poem frequently urges this reader at
least beyond his fears to share something of his delight and en-
lightenment with other readers of the poem, actual and potential.
So this brief reflection of one reader's pleasure at reading the latest
instalments, 26 and 27, of Thomas Kinsella's numinous and en-
trancing *Peppercanister Series*.

Thomas Kinsella, born in Dublin in 1928, has spent much of his
recent life in the USA without losing that sense of inner-city
Dublin in which he was born and grew up. An outstanding poet,
translator and editor, he has never quite attained the popular
acceptance of some of his younger colleagues like Heaney and
Longley. For some readers his poetry is difficult and that seems to
prevent them from appreciating its beauty and power. Indeed he
does demand concentrated and repeated reading if the reader is to
get inside the poem and the poem inside the reader. Yet he remains a unique source of insight and delight in gaining access to
the troubled meaning of life in Ireland, ancient and modern, as
well as in the wider world. His work may therefore enable the
kind of spiritual growth which all serious art offers.

The *Peppercanister Series* was begun by Kinsella publishing
some of his own poems in pamphlet form in the year 1972. The
first of the series, 'The Butcher's Dozen', was a poem written in
outraged response to the Widgery Report as basically a cover-up

of what happened in Derry on Bloody Sunday. Later poems in the series included 'Songs of the Psyche' (1985). At a later time the series was produced by John F. Deane's Dedalus Press, which is responsible for distributing these two latest volumes.

Peppercanister 26 and 27 appeal certainly in title and theme to the contemporary theological ethicist, entitled as they are, *Man of War* (26) and *Belief and Unbelief* (27). Not that the poems are in themselves ethical or theological exercises by the writer or even quarries for ethical or theological material for the reader. As good poems often do, they bring to rhythmic, imaginative and moving verbal expression the poet's wrestling with the beauties and horrors, the truths and ambiguities of crucial aspects of the human condition. In experiencing these poems through repeated readings the reader is changed, if not utterly, at least seriously. Perhaps the writer has also been changed.

Disposing of the Cost
In many ways *Man of War* is the more accessible of these volumes, which is not to suggest that it is in any way an easy read or a superficial comment on the horror and futility of war. Prompted, as an introductory note explains, by an invitation to the poet 'to sign an appeal for the abolition of war', it far exceeds in depth of insight and power of expression the rhetoric and analysis of any simply political or even theological call to disown and abolish human violence and war.

Man of War, like others in the series, is divided into two sections as with main thesis and accompanying 'Notes'. The first section comprises three poems (chapters) entitled 'Argument', 'Retrospect' and 'A Proposal' while the second section, 'Notes', not academic footnotes but seven poems in their own right, offer powerful and particular metaphorical accounts, illustrative of the themes developed in the first.

Belief and Unbelief is also presented in two sections. The first section is untitled with the second bearing the volume's overall title: 'Belief and Unbelief'. And there are less obvious connections between the poems in the first section and those headed 'Belief and Unbelief' in the second. So much for background and structure. Now for the poetry itself, no easy task in enjoyment and understanding.

'A brutal basis in the human species', the first and frightening line in the first poem 'Argument' in Kinsella's *Man of War*. Apart from its argumentative significance for the poem, and indeed for the book as a whole, the line opens us up to the horrors of animal violence in which humans share, but which are then eclipsed by humans' mass destruction of one another. The poetic power and moral thrust of poem and book are quickly manifest: 'But there is a mark not shared with the dumb beast:/ the willed, and mass, occasional destruction/ of others, face to face, of the same kind.'

> The spectacle of other living creatures ...
> organised for self extermination ...
> Would startle and arrest. A just Observer
> Would choose to intervene and save,

Kinsella weaves biblical, cultural and political references to conclude: 'Each aspect of the real as discovered,/ no sooner understood but turned to use/ in sharpening the instruments of war.'

He distinguishes theorists who find war natural and those who 'deny it any basis in the reason'.

'The questioning continues and the waste.'

In 'Retrospect' he speaks of 'a certain grandeur in the past' ...
As the splendour faded /

> the slaughter gained in deadliness and range ...
> in termination,

> delivering a total coup de grace,
> a single phantom with a playful name
> dissolves a city in a bowl of flame.

This history of human self-destruction is followed in the end-poem of the first section, entitled 'A Proposal', with apparently playful but deeply revealing alternatives to 'reach the diplomatic stage direct.

> In oral warfare: arguing the issues,
> Serious, in a game of verbal chess;

The loser underwriting the result
With his own life, in form and in the flesh.

But it seems the slaughter and sacrifice of young lives is required 'for purposes not theirs to understand'. So he would sign
'all protests and appeals for abolition/ of warfare from the world,
if I can find/ where to send them that would have effect.'

So he modestly proposes 'acceptance of the Curse but with
control:' which would allow violence but not killing when the decision would be reached 'in a closed place, between professionals'.

Or- accepting death- eliminate
the element of waste: sending the leaders, …
naked against each other in a pit;
Granting the victory, …
to a lone survivor.

In the 'Notes' the poet moves judiciously between natural
science in 'An insect dialogue' dealing with ants on the march, the
religious world in 'By the dead sea', with its crusades in 'A sleep-
ing cancer', Job in 'The War Horse' to 'Instances from the Greek',
the memories of 'Old Soldier'. The final poem in 'Notes' confronts
us with our contemporary disasters in 'Irresponsible Leadership – a particular case' with no prizes for recognising the prime
suspect, but he has lots of other competitors over the years, centuries and millennia.

a direct behaviour
 centred on self, without self-criticism,
childlike: as if playing with big blocks
and moving them about on immediate impulse

– deploying his huge forces with fixed ideas,
careless of the carnage and destruction;
disposing of the cost in human deaths

and with simple rhetoric and a lack of feeling.

Kinsella, in the hard-edged poetry that is his usual medium, exposes in this volume and with an amazing historical sweep the evolving horrors of all war. No theological appeal could hope to compete with its poetic power in revealing the terror and absurdity of war. No theologian would dare propose his logical and absurd alternatives. Even if he or anybody else does not quite know where to address the appeal, the call to abolish war is immeasurably strengthened by this work.

The ethicist is inevitably attracted to the moral story and moral imperative which the poem undoubtedly contains. That may well be at the expense of his appreciation of its poetic form and power. And Kinsella does offer not an obvious or easy poetic form. Yet it is only by letting the poetic form and power shape the reader's response will he become properly converted to the ethical essence. The quotations cited above give some indication of this close connection between poetic form and moral content. Only by reading and re-reading the whole volume can this reader at least hope to understand, admire and finally enjoy Kinsella's aesthetic entry into the ethics of war and peace.

And the end of all our exploring
To the theologian, the volume *Belief and Unbelief* is less open to being raided for its religious or theological content. Its indirection demands slow, meditative reading which may still leave the reader puzzled about the meaning of any particular poem and its relevance to the volume as a whole and to its title. Kinsella's ambition of creating an open sequence, particularly with the *Peppercanister Series*, offers some help or at least consolation to the frustrated reader of the more difficult parts of the series. Yet earlier volumes such as *Godhead* seem more accessible without preparing this reader for the difficulties and perhaps depths of this one.

The indirection is especially characteristic of the poems in the opening section which, as mentioned earlier, lack the obvious connections with those in the second section which bears the volume's overall title 'Belief and Unbelief'. Given this apparent discontinuity and opacity, the best strategy may be to surrender to the individual poems and perhaps catch 'a distant taste of the raw random/ that walks at the side of Man,/ to unsettle his wandering purpose/ and unfocus his old age.' ('A Morsel of Choice')

This fourth poem in section one confirms the isolation of the narrator in the earlier ones. In 'Novice' he is 'beginning to be solitary in my habits.' His only companion 'in the last light near the river' arrives 'When a pale small body/ landed on a stone near my foot./ ... Exactly the same as in the animal book/ in the old wardrobe in the back bedroom,/ with big grey pictures:'. The 'smell of the old clothes covering the animal book' mingles now with 'a dry ancient smell off the death moth/ – my foot squeezing it and its little glands/ into the moss on the stone'. But which is the novice here, the narrator or the moth, and are both sharing a common novitiate before being squeezed 'into the moss on the stone'?

'Delirium' and 'Superfresh' move from the isolation of the hospital bed to the isolation of the supermarket. For the patient contact is minimal with the doctor, despite 'Our eyes feeding on each other', and with visitors, 'Come to see us sick/ that would not see us well'. So will someone 'please get me/ out of this place'.

The shopper is 'In my leather overcoat, in from the Winter; bearded' and 'A woman ... was asking, in a thick accent,/ where I came from; saying/ that she came from Russia .../ I...told her where I came from./ Her eyes faded ... Our spirits disengaged somewhere over the Alps.' While this occurs 'in a fragrance off the shelves/ of Italian loaves and French boule', there is here as in the hospital more than 'a distant taste of the raw random/ that walks at the side of Man'.

The 'raw random' persists with echoes of isolation in the two final poems through the paired intimacy of love and death. 'Echo' describes the pilgrimage 'to the holy well' when they held hands 'through the heart of the wood ... and told their tales/ as they said they would/ on that distant day/ when their love began.' As they were leaving still 'hand in hand ... she stopped and whispered/ a final secret/ down to the water'. Intimacy yields to isolation for a moment and at random it would seem.

'Art Object' in title and structure appears to escape the 'random' but the intimacy, the intimacy of death, indeed of killing, is the cruel prelude to isolation. Without identifying killer or prey or indeed the nature of the 'Art Object' as painting, sculpture or even poem, the poet presents a careful study of the intimacy of the relationship in its finally isolating destructiveness. 'Her face buried in the live neck, / her top lip pulled back / the fangs dug deep. / She is aware of nothing but the immediate need. / Her young prey is aware / of his part, and accepts it / with panic and protest, but understanding. / Another's need fulfilled.'

The careful crafting in description of the kill, with every word in place, continues into that of the birth and perfecting of the prey to where 'his lot (is) / to be selected at random, and stopped'. A methodical restoration of the scene completes the poem.

What do the randomness, the loneliness and the destruction unto death in some poems presage as we move on to section two with its explicit title 'Belief and Unbelief'? What effect have these opening poems on the reader? Not a comforting effect certainly? An enlightening one? Intellectually or emotionally? One could perhaps detect a certain cleansing, intellectual and emotional, in viewing the animal and human and artistic world. A cleansing essential to exploring authentic belief or unbelief in the following section?

The exploring remains mainly indirect and its conclusion uncertain, although the last three poems might seem to the reader to favour the discovery of belief. The explorer's vision in 'Legendary Figures, in Old Age' has a number of elders shamelessly playing with one another as a woman remarks: 'We cannot renew the Gift / but we can drain it to the last drop'. In the following, associated poem, 'Lost Cause', 'others grey featured and slow' are condemned 'to the wasting of their eternity ... / because they had not / discovered the cause of their complaints'. The eat, drink and be merry group making the best of life while it lasts in contrast to the complaining, indecisive group, wasting not only their time but eternity; two groups of unbelievers?

The ambiguity of the explorer becomes more overt in the third poem 'Ceremony' when he yields

'to an impulse, / growing in the cold mornings / as I passed through the great blank door, / and walked through the high darkness, ... / to kneel at the marble rail, / with my palms together / before the hidden Host'. After 'It is accomplished: ... / I will return through the high dark / among the shadowy believers / to the orderly interests of the day.'

The return from 'kneeling before the altar / under the bowl of blood / with the seed of living light' to the orderly interests of the day does not betoken the end of all exploring as the two following more indirect poems make clear.

'Foetus of Saint Augustine' imagines Monica after his conception when 'the little shape is bent under her heart, / as though examining the terms offered / or examining the carnal basis / for issues of such spiritual complexity, / or as if listening for a breath of wind / that has passed, and might return.'

The 'breath of wind' might suggest the movement of the Holy Spirit at the conception of Jesus but this is no immaculate conception as his parents are invoked 'when they lay together in pleasure, / mouthing each other's names / with eyes half closed, and sighs and body liquids'. So 'the carnal basis / for issues of such spiritual complexity' was truly laid. Augustine himself had enormous difficulty in negotiating between that basis and issues of the spirit in practice and in theory or theology. So had his successors as believers, theologians or saints. And 'the breath of wind' they called the Holy Spirit did not always return effectively.

The poet's acute presentation of Augustine's dilemma over the carnal and the spiritual and that of other believers shows how he shares sympathetically in that dilemma, but does it show how far he shares the underlying belief?

'Genesis', the next poem, is even more puzzling. Relocating 'The beginning ... among the other people, ... near the Northern dark' with similar 'stories ... of exile and dispossession, honour and shame, births foretold or exchanged' offers parallels to the biblical book(s). Yet the hope of a messiah, of a new covenant is eclipsed when 'Fate took shape once, and settled among them. / On a great stone, as a bird with black wings.' From Massada to Auswitz and beyond? Can one believe after the Holocaust?

To judge by the last three poems one can – with difficulty while watching and waiting. In 'Prayer I' the poet 'In a disordered and misguided company', prays: 'Dear God, let the minds and hearts/ of the main body heal and fulfil/ and we will watch for the first sign/ of redemption:/ a turning away from regard beyond proper merit,/ or reward beyond real need, toward the essence and the source.'

This appeal to God for moral conversion of the 'main body' as a signal of redemption takes on a more personal character in Prayer II. 'That the humours settling hard/ in our heart/ may add to current of understanding./ That the rough course/ of the way forward/ may keep us alert/ for the while remaining.'

The last poem 'Addendum' presumes to speak for God's self as revelation displaces exhortation and mystery subsumes morality.

> And remember that My ways
> that can seem in the short term
> mysterious and unfair
> and punishing to the innocent
>
> will justify in the end
> the seeker after justice
> and not the power seeker
> crumpled in his corner.

The Seeker after Peace and Justice

The poetic invocation of the horrors of violence and of war in *Peppercanister 26* must be given its literary due in language, image, rhythm and its consequent emotional and intellectual disturbance of the reader. Out of all that, emerges the aspiration to peace and the invitation to the abolition of war as both inhuman and irrational. Allowing for 'the Curse' becomes a diminishing option if humanity and civilisation are to survive.

Peppercanister 27 digs deeper still but in the same exploratory human vein. ' Novice' 'in the last light', and still enmeshed in violence, becomes the more conscious explorer in 'Ceremony'. The power of the poetry assumes the form of prayer before moving in the final poem, 'Addendum', into God's Book-of -Job-style self-justification.

'… My ways / … will justify in the end / the seeker after justice'.

Peace-makers and justice-seekers are two primary characteristics of the disciples of Jesus Christ, as presented in the Beatitudes in Matthew's version of the Sermon on the Mount. Kinsella's latest two Peppercanister volumes confirm their centrality for human living and perhaps believing.

CHAPTER ELEVEN

Beauty, Art and Theology

For Imogen Stuart at 80

Beauty and the beautiful are the grand elusives of the Western philosophical and theological traditions. With the true and the good, the beautiful figured prominently in that great triad of values which reached from classical Greece to modern and post-modern times. Yet in terms of philosophical and theological analysis beauty was almost always the third and neglected Cinderella sister. All the great masters gave it their attention in differing forms, from Plato and Aristotle to Augustine and Aquinas, from Kant to Kierkegaard, Hegel and Heidegger. Yet it remained the underdeveloped sibling, particularly in theology. Change has occurred and is occurring. Beauty and its theoretical amanuensis 'aesthetics' is enjoying a welcome significance among theologians with the monumental work of Hans Urs von Balthasar, *Herrlickeit, The Glory of the Lord*, playing a leading role. New studies appear regularly and an almost unmanageable library of works such as *Beauty and Holiness*, James Alfred Martin Jr (Princeton, 1990), *Visual Faith*, William A Dryness (Baker Academic, 2001) and *The Beauty of the Infinite*, David Bentley Hart (Eerdmans, 2004) among many others confront the deeper and theological issues of beauty, be it that of the divine creator and creation, of creatures and their creations.

This modest reflection could not hope to tackle the historical and contemporary richness of these works. With its limited personal, theological and artistic resources, it seeks to explore some elements of the interplay between theology, art and beauty as they have emerged in the Christian theological tradition and as they are illustrated in the work of some contemporary (Irish) artists.

Convergences without Definition
Definitions of beauty vary widely and present vaguely. Even

what constitutes the essential components of the beautiful or indeed of any beautiful person, activity or object seldom achieves
universal consensus. Most beauty judgements, it is claimed, are
relative to person and culture: 'the eye of the beholder'. Yet there
is an astonishing amount of agreement on the beauties of nature,
without very much exposure to or tutoring in the differentials of
particular landscapes, trees, plants, flowers, even animals.

Differences in judgement arise more readily and frequently in
facing human beings and their productions. Human individuals,
their physical and mental forms, their behaviour, relationships,
social structures or artefacts all may be bearers of beauty without
any widespread agreement among the beholders. Yet convergences develop through the processes of familiarisation and dialogue as the particular peoples and their cultures open up to and
delight in the perceptions and productions of peoples of quite different times and places, cultures and histories. Without agonising
over precise definitions it seems empirically safe to assert that the
beautiful, and the human capacities to perceive, produce and
enjoy it, are genuine universals – if, like so many other profound
human and cosmic realities, not univocally so.

Divine Origins
For the Christian theologian the ultimate roots of beauty, its convergences and differences, its human perception and production,
lie in the existence and activities of God. The divine creator God
and that God's incarnate and reconciling presence in Jesus Christ,
his still creating, reconciling and transforming (sanctifying) presence through the Holy Spirit, provide the ultimate origin for
beauty, human and natural.

For most theologians, including this one, Creator (divine) and
creation (cosmic-human) are distinct realities, although the distinction and the consequent relationship may be very difficult to
describe. More delicate and difficult in the face of the current task
may be the decision on where to begin: with the vision of divine
creation and divine beauty as adumbrated in the Hebrew-
Christian scriptures and their subsequent developments in theology, or with human creation and beauty as encountered in the

diverse human, cultural traditions, particularly those influenced by Jewish and Christian religious traditions. Perhaps the difficulties may be at least circumvented by proceeding in a truly dialogical manner between God-talk and purely human talk.

The Divine-Human Dialogue

All talk of God is of course human in character. Human talk on this theme of beauty and at this level may, however, be opened up by and to the transcendent-immanent reality of the divine in the creation beautiful.

The difficulties of dialogue are increased by the lack of a precise vocabulary for beauty in both the Hebrew and Christian scriptures. As Dryness lists the various words used in various ways which can be and are translated as beauty, he is emphasising a peculiar biblical strength which at once regards all created things as beautiful in their creatureliness and as deriving that beauty from the beauty of their Creator God. It is on later and indeed more recent theological development of these biblical insights that the dialogue in this essay will be based.

Current Difficulties in Dialogue

The triune activity of God described in Christian theological discourse is clearly very difficult to deploy in dialogue with the humanistic discourse native to contemporary discussion of beauty and the arts. Both forms of discourse are also in danger of sealing themselves off from any other possible dialogue partners such as science or politics and so inevitably from each other. The dialogues between theology and science or politics, as well as those between the arts and science or politics, are for another and more extended day. Yet they are not unrelated in their difficulties and possibilities to the dialogue of theology with the arts and beauty.

One of the real sources of disquiet in contemporary public discourse and indeed in the universities, which should be the home of such dialogues, is the absence of intellectual and cultural interaction which in more classical times might have centred about the concrete manifestations of the true (in religion and science), the good (in politics and morality) and the beautiful (in the arts and the wider world). Perhaps this small effort to promote dialogue between theology and the arts in search of some further understanding of beauty may encourage broader and deeper dialogues in place of the cacophonous and shallow exchanges which tend to dominate the public media today.

Art as Substitute for Religion

An American commentator observed some twenty years ago or so that more people went to museums annually than went to church. Leaving aside how far attendance at either betokens true commitment to art or religion, one might concede that for many people in the Western world, including Ireland, art has become a sort of substitute religious spirituality.

The artistic flourishing which has developed in Ireland over the last forty to fifty years, and well in advance of the economic boom by the way, has more or less coincided with a marked decline in religious practice, whatever about the decline in religious belief, always a much more difficult phenomenon to quantify. The coincidence does not necessarily involve causality or, a more relevant element, lead to substitution. Yet on the basis of personal experience, other anecdotal evidence and the opinions of artists and critics, many people look for their spiritual insight and enrichment to the artistic expressions of poets, novelists and dramatists, to music, painting and sculpture rather than to their traditional religion and its scriptures, prayers and sacraments.

That they should expect and indeed find some spiritual satisfaction in the arts is both a plus for them and a possible basis for discussion about the relation between that spiritual discovery and the spiritual reality claimed by religion and analysed in theology. Here such spiritual claims on both sides will focus on beauty, its basis, perception, enjoyment as well as its role in the full human life.

The Innate Capacity for Beauty

In the current artistic world of creators and critics, and of regular viewers, listeners and readers, despite some pretentious advocates of elitism, the innate human capacity to create and perceive beauty is widely recognised. Of course it must develop within a particular culture, and like its counterpart, intelligence, be encouraged and tutored without being imprisoned in some (intellectually) doctrinaire or (emotionally) rigid system. For developing creators and perceivers the impact of wider cultures has been almost always liberating, expanding and enriching.

In a globalising world such impacts can sometimes be disorienting and disintegrating for all of us. And we depend on the artists among others to enable the centre or, in this situation, the many centres to hold.

Hebrew and Christian Traditions

The biblical stories of Creation in the Hebrew scriptures, and as endorsed and renewed in the Christian, are widely and wisely interpreted as expressions of the divine goodness, glory and beauty and as sources of divine delight. 'And God looked and saw that it was good' (Genesis 1:2; Creation psalms *et alibi*). Human beings in themselves and in their relationships ('Song of Songs', love of neighbour) are the climax of such stories for the Hebrews.

The Hebrew Messiah, as embodied for Christians in Jesus Christ, forms for them the ultimate model and fulfilment of human and all created beauty. 'In him were all things created.' The Hebrew lack of a distinct term/concept for the beautiful, in contrast to the Greeks, should not obscure their awareness of beauty as applicable to the totality of the divine work and of the divine presence, although expressed in their own integrated vision and complex vocabulary.

For Christians the Creation initiative of God continues in the sustaining and healing commitment to Israel and its fulfilment in the person, life and ministry, death and resurrection of Jesus Christ. The historical expression and development of that fulfilment is the mission of the community of Jesus' disciples, the church, in service of the Reign of God to be finally achieved at the fulfilment of history in the eschaton. This crude summary of the Christian theological drama of the world, to adapt the language of von Balthasar, has its three major but interweaving acts: creation, salvation and eschatological completion. Its parallel three major characters, the three persons of the one God, are seldom given such parallel prominence even by theologians. Yet a theology of beauty begins from and returns to that triune God, 'Beauty's self and Beauty's giver' (Hopkins).

Christian and Artistic Ambiguities

For the searching theologian, however, immersed as he is in the human history of this radically divine drama, the dramatic language of these characters and deeds are all too human mediations (rooted in the creation-incarnation dynamic as it reaches towards the eschaton). In these in-between times we can all share in the creative-healing work of the Triune God, but in our far from fully healed condition we are liable to be destructive as well as creative. We remain fragile and fallen, sinners *en route* to redemption and fulfilment rather than already fully redeemed and perfected.

Artists share in the creative activity of God in their more intense way and at a different level. Yet they are also part of the creative-destructive human community. Given their special gifts they may be the more powerfully destructive in a particular area. Beauty is the special care of the artists in developing and fashioning worldly realities from words to sounds to shapes and colours in literature, music and the visual arts. That capacity for beauty can transform some of the ugliest human and cosmic realities into the radiance of a beautiful painting of a Crucifixion or a Death Camp without obscuring the horror of the painting's subject or of the viewer's transport at the beauty and revulsion at the horror. Of course the artist may fail even in his sincere efforts and certainly will fail in his insincere search for the merely fashionable or commercial. Beauty is not separable from truth in art as in life.

Artists are not perfect in work or in life anymore than the rest of us. In this, their inevitable human condition, they reflect consciously or, nowadays more likely, unconsciously the condition of the most ardent disciples of Jesus Christ in their service of the reign or kingdom of God. In theological language, they remain sinners hoping to become or to be made saints.

The Emerging Role of the Trinity
Further probing by Christian theologians reveals deeper insights
into the relations of the divine work of cosmic creation, redemption and final transformation with the work of human artists and
so of the beauty of the Creator and 'his' work with that of human
artists and their work.

As noted earlier, while many earlier theologians and some
more recent ones of the Reformed churches concentrated on the
doctrine of Creation as key to a theology of beauty and its human
creators, Catholics and Orthodox focused more on the mystery of
the incarnation and on the person of Christ. Much contemporary
attention in all the traditions is devoted to the role of the Trinity,
often invoking Karl Rahner's summary remark that the 'economic
Trintiy', the Trinity *ad extra* as it were, is identical with the immàn-
ent, the Trinity internal to God's self. These theologians trace the
emergence of beauty in the cosmic and human world, as well as in
the activities and products of human creative artists, to the presence, power and activities of the Triune God.

In the Prologue to John's gospel and in the letters of Paul, (eg to
the Ephesians and Colossians) the original creation, as cosmic
hymn to the glory of Yahweh in Genesis and elsewhere in the
Hebrew scriptures, is rooted in the Word of God made flesh in
Jesus Christ. The role of Jesus, as Word and Son of God, while emphasised through the Christian scriptures as prophet, messiah, redeemer, saviour, reconciler, liberator and final transformer of
humankind, remains the first born of the original creation and the
initiator of the New Creation.

Echoing Yahweh's words to Moses, Jesus tells his Jewish audience: 'Before Abraham was made I am' and in his farewell message to his disciples he insists 'I and the Father are one'; 'He who
sees me sees the Father.' The early Councils of the church, in affirming the true divinity and humanity of Jesus Christ, in rejecting
any kind of sub-ordinationism or monophysitism, were both emphasising the depth and truth of the incarnation as well as integ-
rating Jesus with the Father in the originating and continuing
work of creation.

The Spirit of God Afresh

From breathing on the waters at creation, to overshadowing Mary at incarnation, to descending on Jesus at his baptism, to empowering Jesus' casting out of demons during his earthly ministry, to Jesus' final promise to his disciples before his death and his final evangelical commission before his ascension, to the descent at Pentecost, the Spirit of God has been recognised in the scriptures as a distinct actor in the historical work of the economic Trinity and so in the immanent life of the God of the Christians, the Triune God. For some theologians it is the inner dynamics of this Triune God which is manifested as the glory or beauty of God in the created universe.

The Trinitarian Structure of Artistic Creation and Beauty

In the creative activities and relationships of all human beings, and in a special way in the creative process of human artistic production (in artistic beauty), the trinitarian God operates through its creative Spirit. This is not readily manifest to Christian believers, even interested and artistically informed believers, still less to the non-artistic or non-believer. Yet serious wrestling with the process of divine creation, in the light of the scriptural witness and the doctrinal insights into role of the Triune God, can shed light on the process of human creation.

In turn, attempts to understand the process of human creation in its inspirational origins, its careful craftsmanship and its independent (of its author) beautiful end-product, reveal a triple movement from (inspired/inspirited) artist through the sometimes crucifying labour towards beauty (echoes of Yeats in 'Adam's Curse') to the visual or verbal or musical beauty born of matter and form. The beautiful dance of the Triune God (*Perichoresis* as some early Greek theologians described it), which issued in creation, incarnation and so in reconciliation and transformation of humanity and the universe, finds a limited, analogous expression and development in the beautiful achievements of the artistically gifted or graced.

Making the Invisible Visible

A more specific and concrete example may be found in that Genesis (1:26)/John (1:1-14) connection already alluded to in which the image of God as ascribed to the first Adam is reinforced and transformed in the Word made Flesh and Light of the World, the Second Adam as Paul calls him. And in the opening chapters of the Pauline letters to Ephesians and Colossians (already cited), the profound relationship between Father, Son, creation and redemption is elaborated further, referring to Jesus as the image of the invisible God. It is in that making visible of the invisible, in the incarnation, that early Christians found their justification for sacred images and icons, and that contemporary theologians feel free to refer even secular beauty to the revealing and praising of the God of glory and beauty.

In many of his poems, Gerald Manley Hopkins spoke of this world as charged with the glory of God, as revealing in diversity the richness of its beauty and that of its creator and of relating if all back through Christ to the praise of God,

> As kingfishers catch fire, dragonflies draw flame,
> As tumbled over rim in roundy wells
> Stones ring; like each tucked string tells, each hung bell's
> Bow swung finds tongue to fling out broad its name:
>
> Each mortal thing does one thing and the same:
> Deals out that being indoors each one dwells;
> Selves – goes itself; myself it speaks and spells,
> Crying what I do is me: for that I came.
>
> I say more: the just man justices;
> Keeps grace: that keeps all his goings graces;
> Acts in God's eyes what in God's eyes he is –
> Christ, for Christ plays in ten thousand places,
> Lovely in limbs, lovely in eyes not his
> To the Father through the features of men's faces.

If 'the just man justices', the artist all the more for Hopkins 'Acts in God's eyes what in God's eyes he is'. In his great poem, 'The Windhover', which he explicitly dedicates 'To Christ our

Lord', the 'Christ' who 'plays in ten thousand places' becomes in this image 'a billion/ Times told lovelier, more dangerous, O my chevalier'.

Christ is the model for Hopkins of the beauty of creation, of the glory of the Creator whom all must praise, of the perfection of the poem and of all artistic achievement, as he writes in one of his letters and implies in so many of his other writings. In that sense he is the outstanding christological creator and critic of the art in his time. The recovery in our own time of the Christ theme, in Irish artists, sculptors such as Imogen Stuart, painters such as Hughie O Donoghue and in his own abstract fashion, Tony O' Malley, and in poets such as John F. Deane, may find continuing nourishment in Hopkins with 'The Christ of the Father compassionate, fetched in the storm of his strides' ('The Wreck of the Deautshland').

The compassionate and creative Father moved beyond creation, sending out of love for the world his only begotten Son. In scripture, prayer and the unending variety of human activity from 'justicing', teaching the disciples all truth (Jn 16) and community forming in the Body of Christ (Paul), the Spirit breathes life and love into the New Creation.

Spirituality and the Sacred in Modern Art
In theological discourse, the role of the Trinity in artistic life and work may sound persuasive, but few theologians are artists or even informed art critics. Von Balthasar would be one of the few really accomplished theologians in our time who was also an outstanding art critic. Perhaps fewer artists still are familiar with or even interested in theology. In the twentieth century, from Kandinsky to Rothko, the less technical and for some commentators less focused term of 'spirituality' is widely used. The term 'sacred' is sometimes invoked in a mediating way although it tends to have closer kinship to specific religions and to theology as the intellectual dimension of those religions.

Without a much stronger formation in the history, techniques of art and above all in its practices, it is very difficult for the theologian to specify the connections between the language of art and the language of theology. Yet for the sake of the theologian and her believing community, a persistent attempt must be made. Otherwise the theologian and the believing community will be deprived of a serious enrichment in their experience and understanding of the ultimately graced achievement of the daughters and sons of God who are artists.

The 'Graced' Artist

Some of that connecting language has been noted earlier. The artist as gifted may without too much linguistic distortion be also described as graced. The gift or grace are of course internal to the person and may often be clearly related to genetic inheritance and early nurture. Yet their earlier origins and later development depend on a further range of gifts from dedicated teachers to unexpected opportunities and even to crucial disappointments.

The biography of a great artist is seldom a starlit story of success. Much great art is born of failure and suffering. A theological reading behind and between the lines can often discern the lineaments of a gospel story, from genealogy list to impoverished birth and threatened infant death to precocious adolescence and obscure early adulthood, to successful public career and later ignominious failure unto death, to hesitant renewed recognition, risen acceptance and transformation in glory. A classic study, as theologian David Tracy might say. An authentic artistic story, as Hopkins and other artists might describe it.

Not all artists fit this paradigm and many non-artists do. Without mixing several categories, the saints of all religions and none incorporate the motivations and follow the main outlines of the Jesus story. As theologians seek to convey, art and beauty in life and work are illuminated for disciples by Jesus consciously and for others unconsciously, as they are modelled and founded in the creation, incarnation, redemption and resurrection of the New Testament. Yet more attention needs to be paid to the human process and product of the artist's work if its evangelical good news is to be accessible even to believers.

The gift of artistic capacity is not always in operation. Artists of all kinds speak of artistic block when nothing seems to happen on page or screen or canvass or at least when nothing further seems to happen and the proposed or already begun has to be abandoned for the present. Inspiration, as it is said, is lacking. An earlier reference to that artistic inspiration or in-Spiriting suggested some reflection of the in-Spirited creation of God. In theological terms it could be interpreted as the human participation in that divine work, its ultimate and inexhaustible foundation. Human artistic creativity will always exist as it is assured of that inexhaustible divine resource. That is our crucial hope for permanence of man-made beauty.

The inspiration initiates the process, not without blocks, interruptions, revisions, even abandonment. And the parallels between the divine creative process and the human, for all its imperfections, bear analogous relations of dissimilarity within similarity and *vice versa*, and persist based on the foundation and participation described above. At the end of a particular human artistic process, and that end may be a long time in coming, as with some medieval cathedrals or even modern ones like Gaudi's in Barcelona or St John the Divine in New York, the work takes on an identity of its own, independent of the artist.

In Search of Artistic Criteria

The artist is then as free to admire or criticise it as any outsider. Criteria for such evaluation of the product as beautiful, for example, depend a good deal on the artist's own expectation and expertise and they may well differ from those of colleagues, critics and public viewers and particularly in relation to different eras and styles of art.

What is offered here as general criteria and artistic values comes from a respectable tradition of art criticism and may help believers and unbelievers in the dialogue between theology, art and beauty. With so much emphasis on the artist and his activity the *objet d'art* may easily be considered as purely the expression of the human artist's mind without any regard for the world in which he lives and work. Even the most self-expressionist of artists, a Jackson Pollock for instance, is shaping and colouring in encounter with worldly materials of paint and wood or canvas and in an already existing art-world. That encounter or dialogue with the material and its world reaches from the cave-paintings of

Lascaux (from 1700BC on) to the church decorations of Matisse and colour abstractions of Rothko. For Tony O'Malley and other moderns any piece of wood picked up at random could challenge him to artistic beauty.

In the longer and broader history of painting, historical narrative and personal portraiture proved the medium between artist and his material. It was this materiality of the painting or sculpture encounter that led many theologians and painters in the dominantly Christian era to find their justification for church and sacred art in the incarnation and ended for example the great iconoclastic controversies of the sixth, seventh and eighth centuries. Indeed the incarnation remained almost the exclusive theological doctrine, as we saw, for the justification and interpretation of art among Christians up to very recent times. The return here to materiality of the arts wishes to elicit some more exclusively human artistic criteria or values.

The first of these values, and we will usually use that term, has been and is known as integrity. In this context it applies both to the artist and the art materials or at least the artist's embrace of the materials as proving suitable to his project and employed by him in a way that respects their character and his subject. The shallow and fawning portraits by a grasping painter for a wealthy patron exhibit none of this integrity. Neither, in the writer's view, do the commercialised or pseudo-shocking products of some of the so-called Brit-school. Here, of course, an amateur speaks and while he might not inhabit the cruder fringes of the 'I know what I like' school, he realises he is ill-prepared to distinguish the truly new and authentic from the merely new and fake.

Proportion and Harmony

In another era and a more classical style, proportion and harmony were regarded as essential qualities of such arts as painting, sculpture and music. With the successive artistic revolutions in the West of the late nineteenth and for most of the twentieth century these qualities seemed irrelevant. Yet as the great artists emerged and their work began to be fully appreciated, sculptors such as Henry Moore, Constantin Brancusi and even the rather forbidding

Anthony Gormley (*Angel of the North*) were seen to have a proportion and harmony at least analogous to more classical predecessors of the Roman or Greek eras and styles.

In painting, where the revolutions seemed more radical and
more continuous even in a single painter like Picasso, the discernment of proportion in figure and harmony in colour and composition is much more difficult. Yet persistent attention to originals if
feasible and good reproductions brings into focus a new form of
proportion and harmony as observable in such different subjects
as Guernica and Les Demoiselles d'Avignon. When Picasso visited
Lascaux in 1930, he said, 'We have learnt nothing.'

A more congenial modern painter to this writer, Mark Rothko,
in his abstract painting, combines line and colour in a harmony
and proportion which can be deeply spiritual and indeed transformative for the sensitive viewer. Irish painter Sean Scully, now
an international star, says he was greatly influenced by him.

In the burgeoning field of Irish art and artists, while many of
these revolutions came late, significant artists have emerged. The
work of Imogen Stuart, stimulus for this essay, combines ancient
Irish and modern European in a range of beautiful works. So do
other sculptors such as Conor Fallon, John Behan and Vivienne
Roche in her own unusual and beautiful ways.

Such citations are born of limited experience and personal
preference as illustrating how Irish artists cope with upheavals in
modern art in their own idiom and with due respect for such traditional values as harmony and proportion. Similar reservations
about my preferred painters should be noted. Tony O'Malley,
Patrick Scott, Louis le Brocqy, Hughie O'Donoghue, Basil
Blackshaw and Sean Mc Sweeney are among those who in the
shadow still cast by Jack Yeats have enabled me to see how the
moderns reflect the classical virtues of art without in any way
simply repeating them.

From Craftsmanship to Radiance
The qualities of integrity, proportion and harmony, do not make a
work of art great. Indeed they may not make a work of art at all
and may never have been intended to. A decent house-painter or

carpenter may produce work embodying all these qualities. As scientists might say: they are necessary but not sufficient conditions for good art work. Yet unless they coalesce to produce what is frequently termed a quality of radiance, and less frequently today a quality of transcendence, which captures the subject of the painting and transforms its viewer by transmitting the vision of the artist, it is best not described as art at all. The capture and transformation of the observer will occur in degrees that vary with the power of the work and its visions and with the capacity of the observer, native and nurtured, to be drawn into the work. For both artist and observer this involves time and concentration. For both, but especially for the artist, it is contemplation or vision in action or better still in interaction.

Aesthetics, Ethics and Theology
These qualities and values of serious art are closely related, as many philosophers have noted, to serious moral values. Despite Kierkegaard's sharp distinctions, aesthetics (theory of art) and ethics (theory of morals) at their most authentic share a close and fruitful kinship. However, a deeper analysis of that kinship and its relation to Kierkegaard's third player in the trio, religion, (and its theory, theology) would demand an essay at least of equal length. So a few succinct sentences on my personal view must suffice.

At the very heart of ethics the attraction exercised by the true and the good reaches its culmination in the radiance of the beauty. In and through that truth (integrity), goodness and radiance, transformation and transcendence eventually await the engaged contemplative. The creative, healing and transforming presence of the God, who for so many may still be unknown, provides the ultimate and theological source of beauty, cosmic, human and artistic.

CHAPTER TWELVE

God as Poem and the Poem of God

For John F Deane

Ours is not a prosaic God. Whatever relation the God of Abraham, Moses and Jesus Christ has with the God of (some) philosophers or scientists, it is not one of the conclusion to a syllogism in logic or the result of an experiment in a laboratory. The philosophical analysis of the possible relation between the empirical world and transcendent Being, the pre-occupation of millennia of thinkers, is still a valid and reasonable intellectual pursuit as partly vindicated in Chapter 6. However some of the questions posed there suggest a wider framework of cosmic reference and human creativity. Such reference and creativity have long been a theological concern of the author and form the focus of this article in tribute to Irish poet John F Deane, who has proved in his poetry and criticism an acute analyst and outspoken advocate of the poetry of our God. He is not alone among his Irish contemporaries in this work. Aidan Matthews is another notable example in poetry and prose, while such priest-poets and writers as Jerome Kiely, Paul Murray, Pat O Brien and Pádraic Daly in English, Breandán Ó Doibhlin and Réamonn Ó Muirí in Irish, continue the poetic exploration of God and religion. Deane's published work embraces a much broader range of themes than those of faith and religion. Yet in Ireland he is perhaps the most prolific, consistent and convincing of the poets who handle religious themes. Much of what I write here is prompted by or even borrowed from his recent book, *From the Marrow-Bone*, with accumulating debts to many other poets and theologians. There is a much larger literature on this topic which I could not even consult.

Faith, Reason and Imagination
Anselm's classic definition of theology, 'faith seeking understanding' still retains its validity although it may be helpful to

extend or better paraphrase it for certain purposes. In this and some other contexts it might be expressed as faith, hope and charity, including therefore elements of uncertainty in hope and of practice in charity, seeking intellectual, imaginative and practical understanding. Such an approach would make explicit the role of praxis emphasised by liberation theologians and theology's relation to the arts, a frequent concern of so many theologians today. Besides it expands the idea of understanding beyond the traditional and restrictive western concept of philosophical reasoning or the even more restrictive recent concept of instrumental reasoning. Introducing the engagement of (political) praxis and the insight of poetry and the other arts into the theological project is not to undermine the necessity and integrity of intellectual analysis but at once to transform and confirm it. For Christians a critical reading of the life and teaching, death and resurrection of Jesus Christ as recounted in the New Testament, reveals his engagement with the poor and excluded, the artistic insight of parable and Sermon on the Mount and the intellectual depth and coherence of so much in John and Paul. The theologian or more correctly the theological community must seek to explore this whole complex in the light of subsequent tradition and in the contemporary context. One short chapter by one limited theologian, however much he attends to his peers and predecessors, can essay no more than a slight sketch of one aspect, in this instance the imaginative or poetic aspect, of the grand panorama of Christian faith and theology.

The Scientist, the Poet and the Theologian

In the frequently polarised discussions in media and academe the scientist, of the hard or soft variety, may be too easily pitted against the poet and either or both set up in opposition to the theologian. While major differences in method and content between the work of the three practitioners undoubtedly exist, they have more in common in internal resources of reason, imagination, sense of vocation and committed (loving?) engagement with the world about them, than is usually admitted. For the purposes of this article at least their sometimes contrived quarrels may be set aside, while the differences are respected and the commonalities cherished. The search for a scientific understanding of the physical world through observation and calculating reason demands in hypothesis, experimentation and verification exercise of the imagination and of the judicial reason in assessing the truth of the results achieved. All this is often motivated or accompanied by the beauty of the object studied and the value or goodness of the whole enterprise to the human community. Such beauty, truth and goodness are the values sought and exemplified by serious poetry although the process may differ, and the balance of the internal resources of imagination and reason be quite different. Imagination dominates, but reason still plays a significant role. Theology as the interrogation of religious faith with its essential companions of hope and charity (in practical engagement) is bound to the traditional transcendentals of truth, beauty and goodness also, although beauty may often be the poor relation in this context. Imagination also has been frequently ignored as in some other human disciplines in favour of a futile imitation of an inferior form of 'scientific' reasoning. It is for such deficiencies that theology needs the spiritual nourishment of poetry in word and metaphor, image and music without neglecting the challenge and truths of science

Prayer, Poetry and Theology
A basic expression of faith (hope and charity) is prayer: a reaching of the mind and heart for the ultimate mystery of God. In many ways this may be better described as conscious acceptance by the person or community of God reaching for them. The initiative lies with God who created us and both inhabits and transcends us. Prayer is our awakening in voice or in silence to this creative and sustaining power. Because our vocabulary labours and our mind falters before this mystery, we are driven to invoke some of the great traditional and oft-times poetry-style prayers from the past. The best-known example of this is the recitation or chanting of the psalms. Anyone with pastoral experience will recognise how often the bereaved will request Psalm 23, 'The Lord is my shepherd' at the funerals of family or friends. This is not simply be-

cause it is one (the only one!) they are familiar with but because of the profound faith and trust or hope it expresses in poetic form, a form that lends itself readily to music. Music is itself often the supreme expression of faith, the highest form of prayer. The internal relations of music, song and poetry may be taken for granted. Great music in origin and destiny shadows prayer and may become a substitute for it as churches become increasingly concert venues and not just liturgical or prayer spaces. Concerts in churches can prove to be prayerful or near-prayerful occasions, depending on the music on offer and the response of the audience. Such music is often 'sacred' music anyway, borrowed from its original liturgical setting. So music might be analysed as mediator between poetry and religion/theology by somebody more expert in the musical field.

The Praise and the Pain
As the first expression of faith (and hope and charity) is prayer, a reaction, personal or communal, of awe in face of Creator and creation, of trust in their goodness and of engagement with their rich reality, prayer is thus the beginning of theology for Christians and perhaps for all believers. Theology moves from the awe and wonder to unceasing exploration only to arrive back where it started and know the place of Creation and Creator for the first time. In its creation poetry starts often in the same place of wonder and awe, although in our secular age that usually stops short at the creation or perceptible world. That is inevitably so for unbelievers although the poem itself may exceed the intent of the poet and carry some readers into a beyond or transcendent realm. The poet cannot simply control or restrict the range and impact of what he has written and released into the world. Of course the theologian cannot control the range and impact of his theology or prayer either which may for some fall short of his intended move towards God and for others exceed the author's conscious intention and his gifts.

And that first expression in prayer will be one of praise or pain and only later the more conventional petition. In their intellectual preoccupations theologians may have failed to pay sufficient attention to these originating forms of expression as ways into exploring human relations with God despite the role of both these ways in that scriptural book of prayer, the Psalms, as well as in so much of the rest of the scriptures, Jewish and Christian.

Praise and pain have characterised so many of the great poets of Christian faith also. The most telling examples in English-language poetry may be George Herbert and Gerard Manley Hopkins who has had such widespread influence on contemporary poets, believing and unbelieving, as many of them acknowledge themselves. Almost all of their poetry is suffused by prayer but Herbert addresses the issue directly in his marvellous poem simply entitled 'Prayer (1)'.

> Prayer the Church's banquet, Angels' age,
> God's breath in man returning to his birth,
> The soul in paraphrase, heart in pilgrimage,
> The Christian plummet sounding heav'n and earth;
> Engine against th' Almighty, sinners' tower,
> Reversed thunder, Christ-side-piercing spear,
> The six-days world-transposing in an hour,
> A kind of tune, which all things hear and fear;
> Softness, and peace, and joy, and love, and bliss,
> Exalted Manna, gladness of the best;
> Heaven in ordinary, man well-dressed.
> The milky way, the bird of Paradise,
> Church-bells beyond the stars heard, the soul's blood,
> The land of spices, something understood.

The complex richness of image and metaphor in this poem gives the reader pause before the mystery. Indeed one is tempted simply to pause at just one metaphor as mediating the mystery and pray with it. And of course it has proved a gold mine for authors in search of titles from Kat O'Brien's *Land of Spices* to Noel Dermot O' Donoghue's *Heaven in Ordinary* to Radio 4's Sunday night programme, *Something Understood*.

From Herbert's seventeenth century English delicacy to the by now at least more weather-beaten contemporary Australian poet, Les Murray, is not as eccentric a pilgrimage as it might seem. His

early poem , 'An Absolutely Ordinary Rainbow' from the collection, 'The Weatherboard Cathedral' focusing on 'a fellow crying
in Martin Place' and the city's reaction, has always seemed to me a
truly religious. even christological, poem. His later 'Poetry and
Religion' is more directly germane to my thesis.

> *Poetry and Religion*
> Religions are poems. They concert
> our daylight and dreaming mind, our
> emotions, instinct, breath and native gesture
>
> into the only whole thinking: poetry.
> ....
> Full religion is the large poem in loving repetition;
> ....
> and God is the poetry caught in any religion,
> caught, not imprisoned ...
> ....
> There will always be religion around while there is poetry
> or lack of it. Both are given, and intermittent
> as the action of these birds – crested pigeon, rosella parrot –
> who fly with wings shut, then beating, and again shut.

Patrick Kavanagh took his inherited Irish faith more obviously
and effectively into his poetry than most of his contemporaries
and successors, however much he influenced them. In poems of
praise (and blame, he was by all accounts quite a cantankerous
man,) he found his way to the creating and beating heart of the
world. 'The One' is one among many of such poetic pilgrimages
through the praised-be beauty of nature to a typical Kavanagh setting for the centre of the world.

> *The One*
> Green, blue, yellow and red—
> God is down in the swamps and marshes
> Sensational as April and almost incredible the flowering of our
> catharsis.
> A humble scene in a backward place
> Where no one important ever looked

The raving flowers; looked up on the face
Of the One and the Endless, the Mind that has baulked
The profoundest of mortals. A primrose, a violet,
A violent wild iris – but mostly anonymous performers
Yet an important occasion as the Muse at her toilet
Prepared to inform the local farmers
That beautiful, beautiful, beautiful God
Was breathing His love by a cut-away bog.

If Kavanagh did not carry the mark of Hopkins, John F. Deane by his own admission did. In his, *From the Marrow Bone*, a Yeats phrase, he attributes his discovery of his poetic vocation to acquiring and reading a collection of Hopkins at the age of thirty. Herbert has also been a notable influence. The first time I heard John Deane speak, he included a reading of Herbert's poem 'Love'. It enters very clearly into the form of his recent peace poem, 'The Poem of the Goldfinch' which also includes his sense of prayer-praise, of beauty and of divine presence.

The Poem of the Goldfinch
Write, came the persistent whisperings, a poem,
on the mendacities of war. So I found shade
under the eucalyptus, and sat,
patienting. Thistle- seeds blew about on a soft breeze,
a brown-gold butterfly was shivering on a fallen
ripe-flesh plum. Write your dream, said Love, of the total
abolition of war, Vivaldi, I wrote, the four
seasons. Silence, a while, save for the goldfinch
swittering in the higher branches, sweet, they sounded,
sweet-wit, wit-wit, wit-sweet. I breathed
scarcely, listening. Love bade me write but my hand
held over the paper; tell them you. I said,
they will not hear me. A goldfinch swooped,
sifting for seeds; I revelled in its colouring, such
scarlets and yellows, such tawny, a patterning
the creator himself must have envisioned, doodling
that gold-flash and Hopkins-feathered loveliness. Please
write, Love said, though less insistently. Spirit. I answered,

that moved out once on chaos … No, said Love,
and I said Michelangelo, Van Gogh. No, write
for them the poem of the goldfinch and the whole
earth singing, so I set myself down to the task.

What mixture of praise or joy and pain is involved in the making
of an individual poem only the individual poet can say. And not
all of them do. Indeed the cost is seldom directly acknowledged
but may be sometimes discerned by the sensitive reader of the
poem or even observed in the poet's voice or face as he offers the
work to the public. For all that this may seldom happen there is no
doubt that the final version of the most praise-filled, joyful and
true poem has involved inevitable birth-pangs. The much labouring which Yeats insists the beautiful demands is for him directly
related to making poetry. And the labour-pains of a mother in giving birth, while later yielding to the joy that a child is born into the
world, as the gospel reminds us, is taken as an apt analogy for the
work of the poet (and other artists). Poets speak metaphorically
but appropriately of their poems as their children. They sometimes speak of the birth-pangs also as Deane delicately indicates
in 'The poem of the Goldfinch'. Yeats seeking a theme and seeking
it in vain or his self-questioning over whether his work sent certain men out to be shot convey something of the tragic labouring
to be beautiful.

More clamorously many of the great psalms are poems of pain.
So is Isaiah's Song of the Suffering Servant. They receive their bitter fulfilment in the Jesus story. His 'My God, My God, why have
You forsaken me' on the cross reveals the ultimate depth of Psalm
22 and of the poem as not just born in pain but in expressing the
profound experience of pain itself. This is the model for Hopkins'
late dark sonnets and for one early, perhaps first serious poem of
Deane, 'On a Dark Night', which also appears in this latest book.
One of the most searingly painful of modern religious poems is
the prison-poem of Jerome Kiely, 'The Leper Mass', in his collection, *A Swallow in December*. It is also one of the most explicitly
faith-filled.

The Making of a Poem and the Making of a World

The making of a poem, or particularly of a collection of poems, involves the creation of a world. The worlds of Yeats or Heaney, or in this context of Hopkins or Deane, are of course complex, too complex and compact for detailed prose description even by the poets themselves. They might fairly tell us to go and just read the poems. Major critics can occasionally be of help but can also be a distraction from allowing the poems to inhabit the reader and so enable her/his world to be enriched and expanded by the world of the poetry to the extent to which s/he is capable.

This partial entry into the world of any poet offers a share of his vision, which will retain the mysterious and unfinished character of all such visions. With reflection, a further labour of love and life, the vision may enable the reader to share even more partially in the poet's process of creating this vision, of making this world. That such a process may be painful has been made clear. That the poet may enjoy the process from first hint in mind or sight or sound is no less true. The mixture of pain and pleasure in the making may continue into completing the poem and finally letting it go. And what its readers, particularly its critical readers, experience may have equally mixed results. The process of poetic creation, the end product of the poem and its world, the release to readers and their reaction, all have particular interest for the Christian theologian as student of the divine Creator and the world of divine creation. The theologian works with the human tools of words and images, intellectual and imaginative processes in discussing the divine. What occurs in human creation then by poets and other artists offers, theology argues, an analogy to understanding divine creation. In crude terms there is at once an affirmation and a negation of the likeness of the human activity to the divine which issues in a transcendence and a transformation of such concepts and processes at the level of the Ultimate Reality we call God. Divine creation, as spelled out in the poetic accounts of Genesis and Job and other scriptural passages, finds a certain resonance and similitude in the work of some of the great artists. There are however enormous differences in free creation of a world *ex nihilo*, out of nothing, and the production from already existing verbal, visual and other resources of a poem or a painting. And the world of such a poem or painting is scarcely to be compared with the immense, complex and finally mysterious cosmos. The artist's process and product still bear resemblance to divine creation, derive from its resources and are dependent on the continued creative sustaining of the creator God. Without that creative sustaining the cosmos would lapse into nothingness, whereas the human artistic object once completed is no longer dependent on its human maker.

Questions remain about how far the analogy between divine and human creativity illuminates either. The continuing and active involvement of the divine creator with his creation as recorded in the Hebrew and Christian scriptures is a critical one. Creation as many theologians and scripture students agree is not a single once for all action by God who then left the world to its own devices. This was the view of the Deists in the eighteenth and nineteenth centuries although it has reduced for many of their successors to agnosticism or sheer atheism. God's continuing involvement is first of all in a continuing act of creation without which the whole project would again lapse into nothingness. Beyond that it includes God's involvement in human and cosmic history which is called providence. And as the spokespeople of the creation, the human community, created in God's image and endowed with the gifts of freedom and knowledge respond or fail to respond to the loving initiatives of God, God is exposed to rejection and suffering. This idea of a suffering God is highly disputed among Christian theologians. As frequently presented in the scriptures and regarded as less threatening to God's transcendence, God is a compassionate God. God suffers in companionship with humanity. This reaches its climax in God becoming human and accepting rejection and betrayal, suffering unto death as way of overcoming human rejection, suffering and death. That victory was established in the risen Christ and is to be shared by all in the New Creation which the Christ event inaugurated. The move from Creation and its Covenant through the call of Israel and the coming of Christ confirms the creative and providential work of God as our past, present and future empowerment in history and the cosmos as we are drawn to the final fulfilment with God beyond history.

Human creativity cannot match in process or product such creative and compassionate power. Yet at their best poetry and other art objects do enable us to share in new worlds and continue to nourish successive generations. There is a continuity of the object's creating and compassionate companionship beyond its first completion and the lifetime of the artist. The artist as noted earlier suffers the pains of creation and these may be continued in his own awareness of the limitations of his finished work and still more in the negative reactions of his audience. Yet the scope and duration of his suffering is limited not least by his death and the future celebration or denigration of his work, unlike that of the Creator God, will be lost on him.

Although the authors be long dead, their work and its influence will not be lost on future generations in the grand tradition of poetry in his language. Such presence and power of human creation in the arts and architecture as in the sciences and technology reflects at its own creaturely level the unbroken creative presence and sustaining power of the divine Creator, the Living God. In recent times there has been an important expansion of the human creative community and its influence in a cultural and artistic globalisation. In poetry this occurs through the closer interaction of poets from very different language and cultural traditions and the appearance of excellent translations, which enable the reading public in one tradition to enter the contemporary world of another while retaining the vision and strength of their own. In the perspective of the one Creator God this reflects the unity of his creation and of his universal creative presence as manifest in the particular and temporal.

'I know that my Redeemer liveth'

The manifestation of the transcendent Creator God in the particular and temporal reaches its climax in Jesus of Nazereth. God's engagement with the world from its creation through the beginnings of human failure, the call of Israel and the coming, as Christians believe, of the promised Messiah and Redeemer in

Jesus Christ, involved divine fidelity to the covenant of Creation and God's 'doing a new thing', 'a new creation'. The labour pains of the New Creation were the birth, the life and ministry, and the suffering and death of his incarnate Son, Jesus Christ. The risen Christ was the witness and expression of that newness which Jesus had preached and inaugurated in his lifetime as the kingdom or reign of God and which John in his gospel had frequently described as eternal life. In the new divine project, the old was maintained, healed or redeemed and transformed. The divine creative power had issued in the radical healing of the older broken and divided world. The tower of Babel symbolising human pride issuing in the breakdown of human communication was overthrown by the gift of tongues at Pentecost as men with languages disparate all understood, each in his own language, the Spirit inspired preaching of the disciples. One of the most potentially divisive ills of humanity had been in principle healed. The New Israel or the New Community established in the New Adam was the foretaste and symbol of the New Heavens and the New Earth for which the whole cosmos had been groaning (Rom 8). The redemption in Christ, in whom as Word of God, all things had been created, was also creation-wide.

The poet and the poem exercise their own limited saving and healing powers, primarily in regard to language, but also in regard to people and even the cosmos. A good poem renews the language in restoring its truthfulness, its honesty of expression, avoiding the false and honeyed words of the courtier and the exploitation of the advertiser or lobbyist. He restores it further in re-exposing its beauty in combinations, vibrant and fresh, at times reviving words too long ignored or inventing new and true words. All of this work enriches the attentive and sensitive reader in self, in relationships with others and in perception of and delight in the world. The redress of poetry, to borrow Heaney's phrase, can affect reader, community and cosmos as reader and community are awakened anew to the beauty and fragility of that cosmos. So poets and poetry play a subordinate and derivative, but for those with eyes to see, a revealing and redemptive role in the divine economy of creation-redemption.

The Mystical Moment

According to English poet and critic, Elizabeth Jennings, 'mystical' is one of the most abused words in the English language. She
asserts this in the opening sentence of her introduction to her substantial study of 'Mystical Experience and the Making of Poems',
entitled *Every Changing Shape*, a phrase borrowed from T. S. Eliot's
'A Portrait of a Lady'. She wishes to confine and define mysticism
in her work by following the usage of Dom Cuthbert Butler in his
authoritative *Western Mysticism*. As she interprets him, 'Put quite
simply, mysticism is the study of direct union with God, a union
which reaches beyond the senses and beyond reason' (op cit, 14).

   In this volume she examines a series of writers and poets from
St Augustine in his 'poetic' prose through the great English and
Spanish mystics to major English mystical poets like George
Herbert to moderns such as T. S. Eliot, Edward Muir and David
Gascoyne and including explicitly non-believing poets such as
Rainer Maria Rilke and Wallace Stevens. It is an astonishingly rich
work and marvellously complements Deanes's *From the Marrow -
Bone*. In the study of individual poets they share only one in com-
mon, the seventeenth century English poet, Thomas Traherne,
and even there they go their separate ways as Jennings concentrates on his poetic prose work, *Centuries of Meditations*, while
Deane stays with his poetry. Their conclusions are somewhat different also as Jennings has little hesitation in describing
Traherne's work as mystical, and Deane opts for mildly mystical
in regard to the poetry. It is, however, in their analysis of the relation between poetry and mysticism in general and within their
individually chosen writers that they largely agree. In fact Deane
makes explicit this agreement in his own introduction. I will
therefore adopt some of her direct comments in her introduction
and her use of Eliot's *Four Quartets* in describing some features of
the overall relationship between poetry and mysticism, before reflecting on a particular poet selected by each.

   The truly mystical poets, according to Jennings and quoted by
Deane, 'were concerned with making direct contact with reality
or God'. One of the aims of her book is 'to demonstrate that mystical experience comes from a source similar to, if not identical with,

that of poetry, but is also itself suitable subject-matter for poetry'. (17-18) ... In her later comments on Eliot, in a chapter entitled tellingly 'Articulate Music', she says: 'The Four Quartets are movements in a poem which depicts the way to an experience of loss of self and union with God' (176). This seems to be the nub of the matter. All serious poems reflect a loss of self in the process and the poem but only the mystical reach union with God. Poetry may be the most appropriate way to express this experience of union with God, to express the inexpressible. Natural ecstatic experiences provide only 'hints and guesses' although poets may often express more than they are consciously aware of or believe in. Hence her studies of Rilke, Stevens and Crane. However, her study of the poetry of twentieth century English poet David Gascoyne, and Deane's study of twentieth century English born but American by adoption, Denise Levertov, offer critical insight into the contemporary challenge of mystical poetry to poet and reader.

At the time of writing, Jennings considered David Gascoyne 'the only living English poet, apart from Eliot, in the true mystical tradition' (190). His identification with Christ in his suffering and his reach towards the whole of suffering humankind give many of his poems and particularly his sequence, 'Miserere', (*Collected Poems*, 89-94; OUP, 1988), a truly mystical dimension

'*Tenebrae*'
... God's wounds are numbered
All is now withdrawn: void yawns
The rock-hewn tomb. There is no more
Regeneration in the stricken sun ...

Thus may it be: and worse.
And may we know Thy perfect darkness
And may we into hell descend with thee.

This darkness which is part of the mystic's experience leads to a cry for faith as the third poem articulates:

Because the depths
Are clear with only death's

Marsh-light, because the rock of grief
Is clearly too extreme for us to breach:
Deepen our depths,
And aid our unbelief.

Jennings here is reminded of Vaughan's lines:

There is in God, some say,
A deep but dazzling darkness.

It is that dazzling light-darkness of God in Christ which Gascoyne inhabits with and for his inattentive contemporaries and which he articulates in so many of his poems.

The 'Shy Believer', as Deane labels Denise Levertov, shares in some of that 'doubt and darkness'. However she has many more assured and hopeful poems of mystical moment, as Deane's choices illuatrate.

On the Mystery of the Incarnation
It's when we face for a moment
the worst our kind can do, and shudder to know
the taint in our own selves, that awe
cracks the mind's shell and enters the heart:
not to a flower, not to a dolphin,
to no innocent form
but to this creature vainly sure
it and no other is god-like, God
(out of compassion for our ugly
failure to evolve) entrusts
as guest, as brother,
the Word.

In 'The Prayer Plant' Levertov charts her faith-journey in the image of a small Brazilian plant, 'with broad leaves that fold up-wards at night into the shape of hands at prayer' (Deane, 234).

The prayer plant must long
for darkness, that it may fold and raise
its many pairs of green hands
to speak at last, in that gesture,

the way a shy believer,
at last in solitude, at last,
with what relief
kneels down to praise You.

God as Poem and the Poem of God

Like 'The Prayer Plant' itself these reflections are endeavouring to move through the darkness to hands up-folded towards the hidden God. The poets and mystics with their religious and secular relations, the prophets and visionaries may discern the poetry of God in nature and neighbour, in scriptural, personal and world history and so affirm, in some analogous sense, God as poet. Indeed their own human articulation of God's poetic self-expression in creation, incarnation and redemption becomes for believers the ultimate source and goal of their poetry. Beyond that lies a further mystery, the internal mystery of God and whether might be thought analogously again as a poem itself. In the recent past I have thought of friends as being in their own way human poems. 'Persons considered as unique poems' has helped me to explore and appreciate their mystery more deeply. Much of what we call revelation of God in the official scriptural sense is expressed in poetic form in narrative as well as in vision, prophecy and song. That may merely confirm God as poet but when we relate to the tri-personal God as Creator, Word and Spirit a certain poetic structure seems intrinsic to God-self. Some Eastern Fathers of the early church spoke the Trinity and its internal relations in terms of dance, *perichoresis*. Dance may well be understood as a form of poetry not in language but in equally gracious and graceful personal movement. Given the transcendent nature of God in three persons as the Creator God, as Word of God and as Spirit and inspirer, perhaps the unity of that God might be compared to the dynamic unity of a transcendent, mysterious poem. To elaborate on that one would need a mystical poet such as John of the Cross.

CHAPTER THIRTEEN

The Catholic Intellectual ...
... and the promise of David Thornley

There is scarcely a more politically incorrect word in current media or even academic vocabulary than 'Catholic Intellectual'. Not that 'intellectual' was ever a term favoured in Ireland any more than it was in Britain. Such pretentious vocabulary was in British terms best left to 'frogs' and 'wogs' of continental hue. That Anglo-Saxon bias has not operated to the same extent in the United States of America, despite its having to face for long periods a certain European, including British and Irish, educational snobbery. Indeed one of the great contemporary breeding- and stamping-grounds of intellectuals from all over the world, but particularly from the English-speaking world, is the *New York Review of Books*. Who is properly described as an intellectual and what s/he does is naturally the subject of disagreement among intellectuals themselves and will be the subject of later discussion.

Whatever the current difficulties about using the term 'intellectual', and the *NYRB* seldom if ever uses it itself, its qualification by the term 'Catholic' or even 'Christian' would be unthinkable for most intellectually serious commentators, even Catholic ones. In their world, the term Catholic has lost any of the visionary breadth and intellectual depth which might be associated with the great names of the tradition from Augustine, Aquinas and Dante to Newman, Unamuno and Schumann. If not dismissed as pious superstition, Catholic refers at best to a particular, narrow and authoritarian Christian denomination and at worst to a sectarian and divisive religious grouping. In Ireland the 'sectarian Troubles' in Northern Ireland combined with the scandal of clerical sex-abuse accelerated an already developing decline in engagement with the Catholic Church.

Large or small 'c' as the case may be, in the self-important

media as in the university, settings of so many would-be intellectual and cultural leaders, Catholicism in its intellectual character
enjoys little respect and carries less 'clout', however much members of theology faculties and institutes or church leaders may
deceive themselves and others.

It is only fair to add, in the present Irish context and more
broadly, that politicians earn no more intellectual respect and that
intellectuals wherever they come from are equally disregarded in
political circles. But all that presumes an agreed account of what
an intellectual is and not just a set of agreed prejudices about who
they are and what their roles are. So it is necessary to attempt some
more detailed description of the intellectual, his attributes and
activities. While this desciption is drawn as fairly as possible from
both scholarly study and personal experience, it cannot claim universal validity.

Intellectual Hospitality
Assuming for the moment the intellectual capacity and industry
which seem essential to such an avocation, the aspiring intellectual
must offer hospitality to ideas and knowledge beyond his immediate ken. Intellectual hospitality, more widely and generously embracing of the strange and difficult than simple curiosity (a necessary component), defines the intellectual life in its vitality and
graciousness.

Intellectual hospitality connotes more than the conventional
open mind, ready to entertain any and every view, however ill-
founded or ridiculous it may appear and without any attempt to
evaluate such views. One person may be and is the equal of any
other, and is as entitled to his view as any other, but that does
make the views equal as factual truth or value judgement. What is at
stake here are intellectual rigour and integrity, not simple prejudice
or feeling. Of course intellectuals may, despite their rigour and integrity, finally differ in their assessment of the facts and judgement
of the values involved. They can do so honourably only if they
begin by welcoming the differing other and his positions and pro-
ceed carefully and critically in examining both positions, of self and
other, to some considered and well-based conclusion.

Integral to intellectual hospitality, then, is a welcome for the other and his ideas, accompanied by a critical examination of both positions in search of the fuller truth. The critical reaction without the welcome for the different and the differer, so frequent at the level of public debate, may readily yield to distraction and personal abuse without any advance in understanding of the issues involved.

As I write this in the USA (Easter,2008) in the midst of a close fought campaign to be the Democratic nominee for the coming presidential election, Senator Barak Obama has delivered what even his opponents, Democratic and Republican, have called a 'profound speech' and a substantially 'new analysis of the current state of the race question in the United States'. Yet despite such widespread plaudits, the debate for which he called is not taking place. Most critical commentators from journalists to professors remain satisfied, after their general praise of the speech's content, to ignore that content and raise questions about why he did not deliver it sooner, or distance himself personally from Rev Jeremiah Wright, author of the earlier objectionable remarks, and not just roundly repudiate the remarks. Even friendly commentators mostly muse on how much damage this will do to his campaign. Of course it will damage his campaign but more importantly it will damage the political, social and racial life of the United States itself if the commentariat refuses to debate the substantial issues as deeply and fairly as he tried to do. One is left with the depressing feeling that intellectual political debate in the United States, despite its boasted freedom of speech and its major universities and publications, is as rare as it is in other Western democracies. And the initial welcome for the different is no more than headline deep.

This example may not be simply fortuitous: 'I happened to be there when it happened.' The failure to deal seriously and critically, in both positive and negative senses, with Obama'a analysis prevented that further phase in intellectual exchange, the creative phase. Obviously Obama had not said the last good word on the tangled question of race relations in the US. At best he had said a new good word and would claim no more himself. He had uncynically, I believe, within the context of the controversy generated by Wright's offensive comments and of his own sensitively worded response, attempted to open a genuine debate in which

fresh understanding and creative action might follow in bring-
ing all Americans closer together in resolving their common difficulties. It is in such hospitable and critical intellectual interchange
that what Senator Clinton has called, (creative) 'solutions' may
emerge and the 'change' advocated by Senator Obama may come
about. And should Senator McCain prove the eventual winner in
the Presidential race, his preoccupation with security could only
benefit from the creative debate which such a significant speech
should prompt.

The creative side of intellectual life and debate is seldom directly associated with political life and debate. Yet the major political challenges such as bio-experimentation, healthcare from HIV
and AIDS to bird/swine-flu, the environment, peace and war,
world poverty and economics in the context of globalisation, tran-
scend individual countries and disciplines. There are ethical, scientific and other intellectual issues which require serious and
extended discussion around the globe. All of these areas require
their specialist and sub-specialist scholars in a range of disciplines,
scientific and humanistic, sociological, ethical and religious, as I
learned over many years of engagement with the HIV and AIDS
phenomenon in sub-Saharan Africa.

Complete intellectual hospitality to the many facts and facets
of this epidemic lies beyond the capacity of any one person and so
does their adequate critical evaluation. Collaboration and team-
work are essential, where the hospitality is not just intellectual but
includes co-workers in allied and quite different disciplines.
Epidemiologists, virologists and other bio-scientists have to col-
laborate with cultural, ethical and religious specialists in many
areas in efforts to contain the effects and spread of this particular
virus. Such containment, with its need for public and political
awareness and action, requires intellectual leaders who can combine with insight and integrity a number of the results of the relevant diverse disciplines. Senior officials from WHO and UNAIDS
like Jonathan Mann and Peter Piot have often provided such leadership in recent years, while visionary politicians like Nelson
Mandela have, on this as on other crucial public issues like human
rights, exercised enormous positive and creative influence.

As polymaths in such a scholarly diverse world as our own are
necessarily extremely rare and because the few there are may not
wish to join hurly-burly of public debate, the intellectuals of interest here are likely to be established scholars in a couple of adjoin-
ing disciplines with a competence in some quite different areas of
immediate public impact. Their reputations as scholars and their
known interest and competence in other (public) areas enables
them to take part in relevant public debates. To be deemed intellectuals within our description they must move beyond their original scholarly concerns to the concerns of the public forum while
maintaining their scholarly and intellectual integrity and impartiality, their unyielding respect for truth, fairness of debate and the
person of their opponents.

This will be all the more difficult to do given the passion for
truth and right which draws them into the public forum in the first
place. How far such frequently named and influential intellectuals as Edward Said and Noam Chomsky or George Orwell, Jürgen
Habermas or Paul Ricoeur from both sides of the Atlantic, man-
aged to combine their passion and their impartiality is too difficult for this author to judge. Yet that combination, however
skewed or unequal, is essential to the true intellectual. These few
sample names are not meant to exclude or diminish the hundreds,
even thousands of equally famous and effective intellectual contributors to the public square over the past centuries in which the
term and so the role became accepted, sometimes at the risk of
death or imprisonment.

More relevantly to most of us, there are numerous lesser
known but effective intellectuals, as defined above, operating in
the universities, in politics often with a small 'p', in the media and
other institutions or quite simply as individuals, who have by
their intelligence and insight, commitment and integrity helped
to transform the understanding and engagement of local or
national communities. Some of these have, on the basis of their
intellectual convictions, promoted or even inspired and initiated
local movements for peace and reconciliation, for environmental
protection, for just economic development at home and abroad
and above all for the educational advancement of the many in all

our countries, developed and underdeveloped, who remain intellectually and educationally deprived. Although they would be the last to describe themselves as intellectuals it is their intellectual capacity and its accompanying attributes that enable them directly or indirectly to promote the true well-being of their societies.

In the discussion so far, intellectuals have been described dominantly as people of serious intellectual capacity and scholarly attainment who have entered effectively and with integrity into issues of public concern. And this is certainly true as far as it goes. However, as with the lesser known and perhaps less scholarly 'intellectuals' mentioned in the previous paragraph, some important and related actors in the public forum may have been overlooked. I refer in particular to the artists of all 'denominations', painters, sculptors, architects and of course writers from poets and novelists to playwrights and literary critics. In his recent book, *Absent Minds: Intellectuals in Britain*, Stefan Collini lists poet, playwright and critic, T. S. Eliot among the elite, as well he might. Eliot did not shirk public controversy in defence of what he saw as right and for the good of society. Artists are by avocation, explicitly or implicitly, shapers of the public mind and mood. The most notable Irish example may be W.B. Yeats, poet, playwright, critic and controversialist, like Eliot but in such different styles. In a quite different artistic genre, that of painting rather than writing, his brother Jack B. Yeats shaped the public's vision of Irish light and colour, of Irish landscape, face and figure for generations.

The Irish intellectual influence of artists is for later discussion. The point to be emphasised here is that many artists have played and still play roles analogous to the roles of more conventionally recognised intellectuals with a background in the academic worlds of the sciences and technology, of the humanities such as philosophy, sociology, psychology and economics. Literary criticism belongs in that school of the humanities and has produced many significant and influential intellectuals as mentioned above. Architecture as crossing the boundaries between the (fine) arts and the sciences and with its monuments persisting in the public sphere across cultures, continents and centuries, has had its intellectual impact in forming minds and hearts, people and politics from long before the term or category of intellectual was invented. The buildings for the new Republic on Capitol Hill, Washington DC, provide one powerful illustration of this; medieval and later European Cathedrals very different ones; contemporary shopping malls more different still.

Musical artists, both composers and performers may be more difficult to classify in their intellectual roles. Yet from local ballads through national anthems to the towering *Ode to Joy* by Beethoven, adopted as the anthem of the European Union, music's public and political influence has been immense. The same public influence could be attributed to religious music from Gregorian Chant and the Verdi Requiem to Wesleyan hymns and guitar strumming religious pop. A more recent and relevant example of public musical impact may be the efforts of conductor Daniel Barenboim to promote reconciliation between Israelis and Palestinian through his orchestral and personal performances on both sides of that great divide and his illustrated accounts of this work in the Reith Lectures on the BBC. Not all of the music that has been influential has had much musical or intellectual substance, but the great classical composers and performers could hardly be left out of the court of intellectuals, given their intellectual endowment and positive cultural influence.

In this rather summary attempt at defining intellectuals and their roles I have of course exceeded the time-span within which intellectuals have been recognised as such. More controversially perhaps, I have extended the categories of actors and activities which might be properly described as intellectual. This may be a personal failing (or virtue) as I find it increasingly difficult to separate in my own life and work the sciences (my original university studies) with their unceasing impact on the world, the study of the humanities through philosophy and theology, literature and the fine arts to social and political studies. In so many of these I remain a rank but committed and persisting amateur (lover) and revel in discovering their connections and their personal and public influence.

The Intellectual in Ireland

The Irish reputation for imagination and for works of the imagination has always overshadowed any claims to scholarly and intellectual achievement. There is substance in such a claim and some good historical reasons for it, but at best it is only a half-truth, ignoring the pre-Christian and early Christian tradition completely, including the works of the Irish monks at home and more spectacularly in Britain and Europe. John Scotus Eriugena (c.810-c.877) was one of the greatest philosopher-theologians of his day and the Irish reputation for scholarship was well established in Carolingian times. In the post-Reformation period, Gaelic and Catholic Ireland lacked access to local centres of higher learning although a number did find their way to centres in Europe through a range of Irish Colleges. Members of the established Church of Ireland (Anglican) had their own University of Dublin from 1592 and produced an impressive number of reputable scholars and thinkers such as the philosopher Bishop Berkeley and the philosopher-politician Edmund Burke. As this theme of the Irish intellectual and scholarly tradition has been the subject of a fine collection of essays edited by Richard Kearney and entitled *The Irish Mind*, and as this essay seeks to ally rather than oppose intellect and imagination, further debate on the topic may be left aside. As some at least of the intellectual exchanges dealt with religion and Catholicism in particular, their discussion may be deferred to the following section on 'The Christian-Catholic Intellectual and his Critics'.

The close intellectual connection between, for example, politics and literature may be illustrated by the work of eminent historian Roy Foster in his highly regarded if controverted *History of Ireland* and his role as the official biographer of W. B. Yeats, two volumes of which have already appeared. Seamus Deane, poet and novelist, has played a similar major intellectual role in his production of the also controverted three volume *Field Day Anthology of Irish Writing*. While recognising both authors (and their works) as major contributors and contributions to Irish Intellectual life, the controversies they generated provoked fresh developments in Irish self-understanding, developments as yet incomplete.

Foster's critique of the standard nationalist account of Irish history was sharply criticised by some of his historian colleagues as one-sided and dubbed by many critics as 'revisionist' in a denigratory sense. In a controversy which still goes on and which played out, for example, in attempts to end the 'Troubles' in Northern Ireland, the 'nationalist' and 'revisionist' versions may be finding a new *modus vivendi*, although history in Ireland as elsewhere is always likely to be a critical intellectual battlefield.

The Field Day Anthology revealed another sharp dividing line in Irish intellectual and cultural life by its almost complete neglect of women writers in the tradition. This alleged machismo among contemporary Irish writers had already been sharply criticised by poet and critic, Eavan Boland, in her collection of critical essays, *Object Lessons*, but the reaction of the outraged women writers on the publication of the *Anthology* went far beyond that. So much farther that they organised a fourth and a fifth volume devoted exclusively to women writers and volumes much thicker than any of the three previous volumes. This controversy and its issue in these later volumes marked in many and more significant ways the culmination of one of the great Irish political and intellectual controversies which really began in the 1960s in Ireland and had embraced *en route* many of the feminist and indeed liberal issues disputed throughout the western world, from contraception to a whole range of women's rights. It was not entirely coincidental that the women's Field Day volumes should be launched by Ireland's first woman President and a notable defender of women's and other human rights in her years as a lawyer, Mary Robinson.

Of course there were many other public issues debated in Ireland in the last century and many other notable debaters. Among politicians former Taoiseach Garret FitzGerald, former ministers Conor Cruise O'Brien, John Wilson, John Kelly and Michael D. Higgins, Senators Alexis FitzGerald, Mary Robinson, John Horgan, Joseph Lee, John A. Murphy and David Norris come to mind as providing intellectual political debate. However, more pragmatic and partisan attitudes and actions usually dominated.

At a further remove from the hot-plates of politics, history and even feminism, the comparatively cool arena of the arts offered the Irish public fresh insights into their own lives and culture. One of the more notable of these was playwright Frank Mc Guinness's 'Observe the Sons of Ulster Marching to the Somme', a brilliant reconstruction of Ulster Protestants in their heady sacrifices in the Great War by somebody of nationalist and Catholic background. A parallel dramatic achievement was that of Sebastian Barry in his 'Steward of Christendom', about a retired officer of the Royal Irish Constabulary, which had been disbanded at the time of Irish independence because of its British provenance and presumed loyalty. As Fintan O' Toole, intellectual columnist and journalist with the *Irish Times*, said on the occasion of the death of that remarkable novelist John Mc Gahern, (I quote from memory): 'He changed Irish society not by prescribing for it but by describing it.'

This could be said of many other Irish artists in the twentieth and early twenty-first centuries. Two of our foremost playwrights, Brian Friel and Tom Murphy, had their initial success with independent plays dealing with the great Irish curse of the twentieth century, emigration. Friel dealt magically with pre-emigration agonising in 'Philadelphia Here I Come' and Murphy dealt powerfully with post-emigration trauma and violence in 'Whistle in the Dark'. From the plays of Sean O'Casey through those of Samuel Beckett to the latest by Conor Mc Pherson and Marina Carr, and including their directors and performance colleagues, Irish theatre has exposed some of the most powerful strengths and weaknesses of the Irish and human psyche and society, one of the true tasks of the intellectual.

Poets have been no less influential and usually in a more indirect way. Much of best and most influential poetry of the late twentieth century has emanated from poets born in Northern Ireland. That 'tight-assed trio of Heaney, Longley and Mahon', to borrow a phrase which Michael Longley had already borrowed for his Inaugural Lecture as Ireland Professor of Poetry at University College, Dublin, earlier this year, have continued to open us up to dimensions of Irish life and that of the broader world, otherwise too easily ignored. Heaney's 'Republic of Conscience', Longley's 'Ceasefire' and Mahon's 'A Disused Shed in County Wexford' stand out among their lyrical and other poetry as powerful social commentaries as well as fine poems. More conventionally, Irish literary critics of the calibre of Denis Donohue and Declan Kiberd have been engaged directly in Irish intellectual life.

The tasks of the Irish intellectual are not sharply different from those in other similar countries. One might, however, criticise the limited role played by the university communities, especially the scientists, while recognising the expanded role of the artistic community.

One last note, on the role of intellectual journals as distinct from professional or news journals. Ireland has never been rich in them and they have seldom lasted very long. Perhaps the potential readership is too small or those interested get what they want in other publications. However, it would be unfair to overlook *The Bell* in its heyday in the forties and fifties and the people like Sean O'Faolain, Frank O'Connor, Peadar O'Donnell and others who founded and fostered it.

The Christian/Catholic Intellectual

It may have been Ronald Knox who said that the adjective can be the enemy of the noun. No doubt as indicated earlier many critics would regard the phrase 'Christian Intellectual' as oxymoronic. Even Christians and their sympathisers might wonder what Christian adds to intellectual at least in terms of the qualities required. The qualities or attributes already ascribed to the intellectual – intellectual hospitality etc – are also proper to the Christian / Catholic species. So are many of the tasks to be undertaken in society. One might however point to resources available to the Christian and unlikely to be used by others, the resources of the biblical and later Christian traditions, in theology, liturgy, prayer and way of life. These may also underline attributes that are not so intimately associated with intellectuals in general and the public tasks they undertake.

Before examining these further attributes and engaging with some of the personalities, it is necessary to consider the possible distinction between apologists and intellectuals. Apologists occur in many domains of human living outside the religious.

Amid the present campaigns of nomination of candidates for the American presidential election, apologists abound for all the remaining potential candidates. As their apologetic endeavours usually do not have much intellectual content, and even where they have, given their uncritical or non-dialogical defence of their favoured candidate, they could not be regarded as the work of intellectuals. Yet some might. Defence of causes rather than personalities might more easily attract genuine intellectuals. Indeed it is difficult to see how they could engage long-term with their society without supporting the truth and justice of significant causes or movements. In this line Said, Arendt and many unnamed here became apologists for the historical truth about totalitarian, colonial, ethnic or economic oppression, for example, and the parallel contemporary cause of freedom.

Christian apologists as a class originated in Christianity's second century in response to criticisms by Roman critics. While their work was intelligently and often quite fairly presented, it would not be appropriate to describe it by what, as we saw, is really a modern term, intellectual. Given his intellectual capacity, his range of interests, his sheer erudition and the volume of his work, St Augustine must be included in any list of the world's great intellectuals even modern style. But his work as a bishop inevitably had an apologetic flavour in its defence of Christianity. His famous *Confessions* would be read as an apology for his own life but the bulk of his writings were directed to the public square of his time in criticism of its short-comings and its need of the saving truth of the Christian faith. His legacy to later generations of Christians was by no means all positive but his genius and commitment to truth cannot be denied. The same might be said of Thomas Aquinas, although his temperament allowed for a a just integration of such different thinkers as Augustine and Aristotle, a more balanced address to the 'gentiles' and a critical integration of natural and revealed truth. His close contemporary Dante transposed this well of truth into the splendid poetry and prose which marked the imaginative high-point of Christian intellectual life.

However, for our purposes and our times one point needs to be clarified. The Christian intellectual as distinct from the intellectual in the church, is engaged primarily in dialogue with the world about him. He is focused *ad extra*. This will have repercussions *ad intra*, within the church but that is not his main concern as he seeks to use the intellectual resources of Christianity in dialogue with outsiders. In using these he will sometimes at least be acting defensively or in an apologetic way. So long, however, as he is faithful to the truth and fair to the outside partners, he can be a true intellectual.

The thrust of his tradition emphasises qualities that may be ignored outside it. The first of these is humility. All great intellectuals are humble before the truth and behave with humility towards their critics and opponents but it is to be particularly expected of Christians. The arrogance of some Christian and other commentators of the 'left' or 'right' is bound to have a blinding effect on themselves in their pursuit of truth and make it impossible for others to enter into dialogue with them. Many Christian fundamentalists, whatever their intelligence and pretensions to scholarship, fall into this category. So do other fundamentalists, both religious and non-religious. It is very difficult, for example, for a believer to initiate any real dialogue with someone so arrogantly and often ignorantly dismissive of religious belief as atheistic biologist Richard Dawkins.

The Christian engagement with society should always be characterised by compassion. So should that of the Christian intellectual. He will use his intellectual gifts and Christian insights to analyse the lot of the marginalised or poor, and its causes, as a contribution to a more just and free society. This may appear to make him partisan but he will be seeking the underlying truth of the structures of society in order to promote its common good.

One last attribute ought to be required of the Christian intellectual that might be neglected by others. Aware of human limitations, enshrined in the theology of sin, the Christian recognises that no one person is absolutely right about everything in his own specialty, still less as that specialty impacts on a complex and ambiguous world. So he will be open to compromise or at least tolerance of difference while seeking personal reconciliation with opponents. Such personal reconciliation within society, without surrendering commitment to the truth, is essential to a peaceful and humane society. This for the Christian is the only limited realisation possible in history of the reign of God which Jesus preached and inaugurated.

In early student days, *The Intellectual Life* by French Dominican, A. D. Sertillange, was a significant read. The much later book, *The Christian Intellectual* by American Lutheran theologian and historian, Jaroslav Pelikan, was only the second study dealing directly with some of these issues which came my way. They have long been forgotten and, as far as I can tell, have had little enough influence on this essay or on my intellectual life generally.

John Henry Newman, in his lectures on 'The Idea of a University', his *Grammar of Assent* and his *Apologia pro Vita Sua* among other writings offers classical exemplars of the work of the Christian intellectual to which one frequently returns. In a narrower more regular apologetic sense *Mere Christianity* by C. S. Lewis has proved to be both a very intelligent introduction to and defence of Christian faith. However the outstanding Anglican intellectual of our times must surely be Archbishop Rowan Williams of Canterbury, despite his sometimes opaque style and occasional misjudgements, as in his recent reference to the introduction of some elements of Sharia law into the British system – not unlike the misjudgement of the highly intellectual Pope Benedict XVI in his reference to Islam and violence in his address to the University of Regensburg a couple of years back.

The term intellectual was always more at home in French culture and among French writers. Two of the outstanding Catholic intellectuals of the twentieth century were Gabriel Marcel and Jacques Maritain. Simone Weil may have been even more influential on Catholic thinking. She was never actually baptised but had become very deeply Catholic. All three differed greatly in their interests. Marcel's existential personalism helped develop Catholic dialogue with contemporary philosophical movements, while deepening Catholic understanding of the human person and both the dignity and the fragility of its existence. Maritain's revival and renewal of the philosophical tradition of Aquinas introduced it to

modern thinking about human rights, a more complete human-
ism and even philosophical thinking about the arts. Simone Weil
was at once the most practical of philosophers, working in factor-
ies and espousing certain Marxist views and the most metaphysical. Her direct public engagement as a thinker and worker is likely
to be an inspiration to fresh generations of Catholic thinkers.

Maritain worked quite a lot in the United States and developed
his thinking on one of the major concerns for Christians in that nation, the separation of church and state. The distinction between
state and society which he emphasised restricted the state's capacity
to control citizen's lives and opened the way for his analysis and
promotion of human rights, among them the right to religious freedom. This was key break-through for Catholic thinkers at Vatican II.
However, the main architect of the Council's *Declaration on Religious
Liberty* was American Jesuit, John Courtney Murray, who had been
banned from publishing on this issue by the then Holy Office (now
the Congregation for the Doctrine of the Faith). Murray was undoubtedly one of the great Catholic intellectuals of his day. In a
quite different domain Dorothy Day's writings and engagement
with the poor, while not of the same intellectual depth as that of
Simone Weil, gave a power and direction to Catholic social thinking and action which anticipated the work of the Latin American
liberation theologians in the later 1960s and subsequently. Gustav
Gutierrez, Jon Sobrino and others offered a new basis for intellectual
investigation of the faith in society with their insistence on prior
engagement with the poor. The priority of praxis and the option for
the poor has had enormous influence on all Christian action and
reflection from feminism to black theology, from South Africa to
South America to the southern states of the USA.

Before the Catholic Liberationists, Protestant theologians like
Reinhold Niebuhr had, out of his experience as pastor in Detroit
during the depression, made serious intellectual and practical
contributions to social theology. His brother Richard and others
were also engaged in this project of what Reinhold called
Christian Realism in politics. A quite different line was later pursued by theologians such as John Yoder (Mennonite) and Stanley
Hauerwas (Methodist) whose social emphasis concentrated on

peace as the way to justice. In this they opposed the Niebuhrs' line but were in agreement with Catholic thinkers and activists such as Dorothy Day and the Berrigan brothers.

Beyond politics, American theologians such as Paul Tillich and Jesuit critic, William F Lynch entered into serious engagement with culture and the arts. Indeed Richard Niebuhr's work, *Christ and Culture* remains something of a classic in this area. Daniel Berrigan is a poet as well as a peace activist and his poetry had the kind of intellectual impact on society that good poets always have. Fine novelists such as Flannery O'Connor and Walker Percy, while not propagandists, let their Catholic background have its own impact as have later novelists like Mary Gordon.

This extended discussion of American thinkers and writers seemed justified in the light of that country's vibrant intellectual life in recent decades and my own exposure to it. Yet there is much that must be passed over in the American churches and still more in the intellectual life of churches around the world, including Ireland. However, it would be unfair to pass over the contribution of literary critic, Peter Connolly of Maynooth who made a critical contribution to the debate on book censorship and suffered in consequence. Other Irish people who showed intellectual courage in face of authority will emerge in the following sections.

The intellectual in the church
In the previous section the focus as announced was on dialogue between the Catholic-Christian intellectual and the wider society. In this section the emphasis will be on the role of the intellectual internally to the church(es). The distinction is not always valid, as the example of John Courtney Murray would have illustrated. And it applies more obviously to the Roman Catholic Church with its closely structured unity than to many other more loosely organised churches. However, it is a helpful distinction in many ways and prompts some consideration of further attributes befitting to the intellectual with this primary vocation. Of course all the attributes and qualities of the true intellectual already discussed are still required in this instance. And the additional ones listed here apply in their own way to all intellectuals.

The first of these attributes is courage. All intellectuals have need of it from time to time. In the church, and particularly in the Roman Catholic Church with its strong tradition of authoritative teaching and of teaching authority, it is particularly necessary. It should, however, be a thoughtful courage arising out of personal conviction and awareness of ecclesial or social need. Thoughtfulness in this sense is never calculating self-service and the audacity to speak the truth should not be tainted by arrogance. Speaking the truth in love is more than a Christian or church requirement but it is certainly that. To conscience first and then to the church, as the Newman phrase has it. Indeed the courage to speak is demanded by fidelity to the church itself in such circumstances. Courage and fidelity are true marks of the intellectual's activity in the church. They do not guarantee the truth of that speaking or its reception if true. The negative reaction of church authorities or other church members to the faithful and courageous intellectual contributions of theologians and others within the church should be respected, even when not offered, in a spirit of dialogue. Retiring into the role of victim is no more acceptable within the church than the adopting of the role of victimiser. In the light of the Cross, the Christian, intellectual or no, should recognise that such roles are no longer appropriate. That does not mean that either role has simply ceased to exist within the church.

In the theological and pastoral developments finally adopted at Vatican II, the critical role of church intellectuals, mainly theologians, was properly recognised, although many of them had been censured in the decades preceding the council. Rahner and Congar, Courtney Murray and Chenu had all experienced the journey from suspect outsider to approved insider as the council Fathers worked through the council agenda. Of course the council was still only a stage in the historic journey of the church as a pilgrim people. There were further distances to travel and need of the insights of other theologians and intellectuals in that continuing journey, Some of these have also suffered for their courageous search for the fuller truth. Edward Schillebeeckx, Hans Küng, Charles Curran and a range of liberation and other theologians have had to endure disapproval by church authorities without wavering in their fidelity to truth or church. It will ever be so as both authorities and intellectuals struggle honestly to protect, develop and promote Christ's gospel truth.

In Ireland the difficulties have been less apparent but then so have the developments. However, theological and scriptural scholar-intellectuals like Gabriel Daly, Sean Freyne, James Mackey, Terence McCaughey, Dermot Lane, Vincent MacNamara, Donal Dorr, Denis Carroll, Sean Fagan, Patrick Hannon, Linda Hogan and many others have contributed enormously to the thinking and knowledge of the Irish church despite the occasional negative reactions. In other disciplines and intellectual spheres the work of Brendan Devlin, Margaret Mac Curtain, Patrick Masterson, Mark Patrick Hederman, Michael Paul Gallagher, John O'Donohue, John Moriarty and Peter Connolly have left their intellectual mark on church and society. The intellectual life of the Irish church, if often lacking in drama, has not lacked for substance.

The Promise of David Thornley

My association with David Thornley, the thirtieth anniversary of whose death we remember this year, 2008, began shortly after I started to teach at Maynooth in 1960. In the mid-fifties I had been a member of a socially and politically concerned group of young intellectuals and others called Tuairim. On my return after I had finished my further studies, I reconnected with the group. David was a prominent member if not already its chairman. We quickly became friends. In the following years I became involved with a society for Catholic students in TCD known as the Laurentian Society. With many concerns in common, our friendship developed. At one stage he lectured on politics in Maynooth, ironically as substitute for the very conservative Jeremiah Newman who had become president. Unfortunately I was away on sabbatical leave when he died and so missed his funeral. For that and other reasons I am delighted to have this opportunity to pay tribute to him.

In intellectual, academic, media and political terms David Thornley died far too young. However, his many achievements in so many areas indicated what in later and more mature years he might have accomplished. In the context of this essay on the role of the self-consciously and socially engaged Christian and Catholic intellectual, his gifts and ambitions might be best handled as promise of what is still possible and necessary in Irish life. He lived in what it is now considered a narrow and conservative cultural, political and religious ethos. His commitments and activities were directed to breaking out of that. However, whether he was lecturing in Trinity College (or for a short time in Maynooth), presenting television debates, speaking in the Dáil or singing in the Westland Row Church choir, David kept very different strands of Irish life, including the Catholic strand, in communication. The critics of the 'narrow' ethos of that time are often blind to the narrowness of the dominant ethos of today where religious and particularly Catholic concerns and resources are ignored in public debate. The promise of more fruitful communication and dialogue which David Thornley among others embodied for a short time could and should be revived for the health of the nation as well as of the church.

PART III: IN WINTER LIGHT

CHAPTER FOURTEEN

The Burying Priest: District and Circle

In Memory of Sean and of all the others
buried in pain and recalled in gratitude

The three-year-old who recognised the visitor to her granny as the 'christening man' (of her baby sister) is undoubtedly too sophisticated by now to describe him as the 'burying priest', even if she has witnessed him in that role and for her granny also. These two roles of a priestly life shape the crucial poles of every Christian life as we pray 'may he/she who died with Christ in baptism be raised up with him in resurrection'. As the second pole in one's own personal and Christian life draws perceptibly nearer, for the parish-less priest the burying of family and friends becomes the more frequent role with the baptising role less frequent, although still far from dormant. In theological reflection, the two remain intertwined as matters of life and death, indeed of living through dying. However, in this instance there will be more focus on earthly dying and burying as way to eternal living, for it is so Christians hope and trust.

Parish-less as he is in retirement and as he was during a mainly academic life, this priest had and has his own circle of family, friends, colleagues and acquaintances to whom he ministers in various situations including illness, death and grieving. He has his own territory also although it is not to be geographically defined. Indeed no priest's geography ever is. But this priest's territory is more a district of the mind, imagination and feeling developed through his family, his academic work and social causes, and sometimes by chance (providential) emotional relationships. Invoking as sub-title of this short reflection the title of Seamus Heaney's latest volume (itself a borrowed item) may not appear then as simply contrived or even headline-hunting, if expressing the mind and mood and movement of this burying, journeyman priest can shed some light on the mysteries of human dying and grieving.

Early Induction into Death

Long before priestly ordination the future priest visits the painful district of human death and dying; joins the cemetery circle of grieving family and neighbours. Childhood funerals vary from the deeply shocking to the unbearably sad. Be it Seamus Heaney's four-year-old brother, in his 'foot for every year' coffin, to Timmy's thirty-six-year-old father killed in an aircrash, the mourning melody lingers. And without such searingly close experiences to remember, this burying priest can still call up the painful loss of cousins and schoolmates of his own years as well as beloved aunts, uncles and neighbours buried before their due time in his early years. All that helps prepare for the more radical encounters of later life when he must walk the mourning district as liturgical leader and comforting companion.

Liturgical Leader

Liturgical leader is a rather forbidding term for the kindly, pastorally engaged and fatherly figure usually expected to conduct Catholic funerals. The term Catholic or Christian funeral is more pastorally loving and theologically inclusive of those who have been baptised, have lived at least part their lives as active in the faith and whose relatives desire it. The question about who is entitled to a church funeral is the wrong question, with the wrong terms of 'church' for Catholic/Christian and 'entitled' for 'grace'. Two of the great graced public and Catholic funerals of the last year were those of John Mc Gahern (an implicit Catholic if ever there was one) and Seán Mac Réamoinn, one of the great explicit Catholics, many of whose friends were not, or no longer regarded themselves as such, although some of these latter spoke in loving and admiring terms of his Catholicism.

If as happens less frequently nowadays the priest is far too young to appear fatherly, a brotherly style care may be even more acceptable, particularly at the funerals of those who have died young by our human calculations and sometimes tragically. In

either case, the father- or brother-priest may be fortunate enough
to have in family or parish creative lay-persons who provide
effective leadership at least in preparing the liturgy, from wake and
removal to readings (with suggestions for the homily perhaps),
gifts and tributes at the Mass to final cemetery ritual.

One of the great liturgical tasks usually denied to the priest,
but frequently in imitation of the gospel accounts carried out by
women for Jesus, is the immediate preparation of the body of the
deceased. It should at least be performed in the presence and with
the anointing of a priest if reverence for that gift of creation and
grace, the dead human body, is to be taken completely seriously.
Is this just another cultural instance of recognising the female
familiarity with and care of the human body at birth and death, as
did the women at the tomb of Christ and the male distaste for it
and fear of it? With that gospel precedent, should women be
official (ordained) ministers for the dying and the dead? Or is all
this now just the surrender to a secular professionalism, however
'believing' the undertakers of this task may be in themselves?

For all that, the burying-priest must take his own responsibilities fully seriously and exercise his own creative leadership at
least from the final illness to the concluding interment. It is above
all with the liturgical style, pastoral sensitivity and theological
meaning of that journey that this reflection is concerned.

And the most difficult is faith

The liturgical elements, the ritual of anointing and final communion, the prayers for the dying and the immediately deceased, are
with a certain flexibility clearly provided by official ritual and
local custom. And in today's circumstances, from hospital crisis
to roadside or other accident, not always easily applicable. For the
attendant priest and ultimately for the burying priest and for all
intimately involved, faith, hope and charity must give life to the
ritual provisions. And the most difficult of these is faith.

At the bedside of the still conscious but rapidly weakening
dying person, conventional prayers have their role. And the
priest has the advantage of access to prayers ritually prescribed.
Yet the sense of losing contact for ever with that person and the

darkness, bleakness and coldness which that will immediately involve, begins to undermine the connection and communication which the prayer had promised not only with the dying companion but with his God. Some death-rooms with their waves of vocal prayer can remain sources of comfort, but are they always also sources of faith? This is often the accompanying priest's most painful burden. In the insightful words of the Kilreekle bartender commenting on the cheerful English chappy's question to the local curate as the curate sipped his pint: 'Sure if he doesn't believe (in the afterlife), aren't we all ...?'

Crude for the visitor, even cruel on the curate, but reflecting a recurrent and tormenting question for the burying priest not only in regard to the faith of the many he seeks to comfort and serve on that dying and funeral journey, but also in regard to his own life journey unto death. And it is, implicitly at least, that life-death journey of his own that he has to traverse each time he conducts a funeral, even when grief at the loss obscures his own self-concern or the distractions of other sorrows or joys leave him detached from the present.

Faith and the varieties of dying
'S/he died peacefully in her sleep' is the frequently consoling report of bereaved family and friends. It is perhaps the hope of all of us. And it is certainly less distressing for the immediate audience to hear death announced in such terms. But death is still death, the absence of life, the cessation of response and the emptiness of companionship. And the continuing one-sided loving becomes a deeper source of sorrow.

However peacefully she died and now rests, the un-peace of those left to mourn is not quickly allayed. Into all this and more the priest in attendance, particularly the priest-friend, must learn to enter. The 'more' occurs in the more tragic circumstances of young or unexpected death above all and by the violent death of accident or suicide or, less frequently but more searingly in our circumstances, of homicide. On such violent occasions the priest and/or the police may be left to break the news and the family hearts.

A New Kind of Darkness

Entering into the mourning darkness beyond the helpless 'what can one say?' or the too easy and so unconvincing 'She is with PJ and Frank and Pearce in Heaven', the priest encounters the inadequacy of his own faith. He too must let the absence disturb him and the darkness envelop, while he maintains his loving support of the bereaved. Loving them must never involve misleading them about his own settled convictions or present uncertain state of mind. In the loving and supporting the darkness becomes less unbearable, the absence less painful. By surrendering to their distress, the priest is strengthened in his own.

Such loving surrender is not only a source of consolation for all but may become a baptismal font of fresh faith for the shaken priest. He is loved into trusting and believing in new ways by the God who seemed more absent than the deceased, by the emerging presence of that God in the love of the bereaved for one another and for him, and in the loving remembering of the lost one.

Ordinary tasks in mourning time

As the remembering and reminiscing replace the first shock of death announcement, and the practicalities of funeral arrangements take over from the paralysis of first grieving, a solidarity of care and commitment draw mourners and minister closer. Faith-questioning does not disappear for most but it is put on hold as the ceremonies are planned, music and musicians, hymns and singers, readings and readers chosen, gifts and gift-bearers settled and the more ordinary tasks assigned – as if any participatory task in the burial of a loved one could be described as ordinary.

Contacting the undertaker, selecting the coffin, church and cemetery, fixing times and other funeral responsibilities such as who carries the coffin when and where, flowers and newspaper notices, all these detailed tasks of the final journey of farewell are laden with meaning, and sacred meaning at that. However, the stubbornness of things, times, places and people may frustrate and irritate the assignees, as planes are late and fog affects local travel and Aunt Mary takes suddenly ill. However routine they may be for the professionals, the holy-making and saving power of all these practical proceedings is not to be denied. To ensure that, minister and mourners must be constantly alert to the sacred trust of their roles in mourning and burying their friend.

That alertness, in itself a form of prayer or implicit act of faith, is mediated through the deceased in memory and final bodily presence. Reverence for his body and caring attention to its final committal in cemetery or crematorium expresses awareness of the dignity and sacredness of human being and body, and indeed of the creation and its traditional elements of earth and fire. It would be asking too much of the sorrowing congregation to keep in mind or even to be reminded repeatedly of such profound associations. The priest or minister should meditate over the funeral days on these dimensions of Christian burial and by his presence and de-meanour, if not always by his words, mediate them to the believing, half-believing and unbelieving people, that make up most funeral congregations today.

Of doubt and faith

This naturally puts extra burdens on the burying priest. Given his own at least occasional hesitations and doubts, how can he expect to embody in his *persona* and action such far-reaching regard for the dead and to mediate it to the living clustered about him, in their varying degrees of belief and unbelief? An unbelieving friend to whom I voiced these difficulties once remarked: 'On the occasion, what matters is what you, the presiding priest, believe.' Maybe but that does not necessarily erase the doubts of priest or people.

The parish-less priest may have more difficulty here because he is not regularly engaged in funerals and not regularly enriched by the simple and strong faith of at least some of the congregation. To compensate for this, he should have or make more time for preparation in prayer and reflection on the mystery of dying and on the uniqueness of this particular person and her/his death. Ideally this burying priest should be dominated by the life and death of the deceased person from first hearing of the death to the actual burial. Through these days, with their appropriate inter-ruptions for ritual and companionship, he may be able to work through his own fears and anxieties, his own faith limitations, and his inhibitions about speaking beyond death and into resurrection.

A mystery too far
While the homily is only one of the many vocal performances of prayer, ritual and song which every funeral includes, it is more exposing of the priest's love for the departed and her family and friends, of his hope for new life for all of them and of his faith in resurrection. This last is the most difficult and the most tempting to avoid and not for altogether unworthy reasons.

The banal rehearsing of the church's official teaching can be easily dismissed by the mixed congregation he faces, even by some of the believing. For them too it may be a mystery too far. To have lived a good life here is now for many the height of their expectation. Resurrection does not for so many practising Christians match any reality they can imagine. Their immediate consolation lies in the honest and honourable well spoken tribute to their lost one, and that can lead the priest and people into marginalising any further questions. During the funeral days, but also in his longer journey, the priest has to face these further questions in himself and for his people. For the parish-less priest at least the funeral days intensify the questions and so he needs a lot of quiet in these days, making them equivalently into a mini-retreat.

From the Districts of the Dead to Dante's Paradiso
Dante's *(Divine) Comedy* is justly regarded as one of the greatest literary works of Western civilisation but also as a supreme expression of the Christian vision of life and death and life after death. Together with the resurrection narratives and their predictions / anticipations in the gospels, and the theological visions of Paul in his letters, Dante's poem offers endless material for literary delight and theological insight. It also represents a serious faith challenge to priest and people, particularly at funeral celebrations. The traditional teachings on hell and purgatory, brought to such dramatic life in his *Inferno* and *Purgatorio*, have become a focus of intense contemporary controversy among even commit-

ted, informed and thoughtful believers. Such controversies have been complicated and intensified by the recent official abolition of limbo by the Vatican, (home, for Dante, of the great pagan poets and philosophers for example) and by Pope Benedict's recent re-habiliation of hell (home, for Dante, of some popes). Funeral homilies are not the occasion for developing or attempting to settle these controversies – especially when to so many believers after-life itself is being questioned. Purgatory gradually going the way of limbo, and hell regarded as incompatible with an all-merciful God, such debates must be carried on elsewhere.

In the immediate context of a Christian funeral, whatever about more remote background meditation, Dante's First and Second Poems provide little help to priest, preacher or people. *Paradiso* must be the focus, not primarily in Dante fashion, but in more directly evangelical and Pauline terms. In the dialogue between the Christian scriptures and human experience which all real liturgy and preaching involves, poetry and painting and other products of human creativity can provide important stimulus and guidance. Few if any of these will be at the level of Dante's masterpiece, frequently described as the most admired and least read of literary masterpieces, particularly by some of its most vocal advocates.

Without the resurrection the story of Jesus would be merely a *tragoedia* in ancient Greek mode and not the *Commedia* which Dante originally entitled it. And without the resurrection of Christ and its offer to all humanity the story of that humanity would also end as simple tragedy through natural extinction or collective self-destruction. Former Catholic and successful modern novelist David Lodge, in his *Paradise News*, a novel of the late twentieth century, has his chief protagonist, agnostic theologian Bernard Walsh, bang on in mocking vein about the after-life in discussion with his dying aunt. 'It's remarkable,' he says, 'how many modern theologians who have rejected the orthodox eschatological scheme feel free to invent new ones that are just as fanciful' (p 259). And many non-theological believers often prefer to avoid such discussion altogether. The better option, perhaps, but not really available to the conscientious burying priest.

Struggling as he must with the difficulties of believing and still more of imagining the New Life of resurrection, he stays close to the scriptural texts, is ever alert to the penetrating insights of believers and theologians, and enlists when he can the joy and beauty of the great artists such as this poem-prayer taken from Dante, *Paradiso*, Canto XXXIII, in translation by Seamus Heaney:

O Supreme Light, elevated so above
What mortal minds can rise to, restore to mine
Something of what You were when shown forth,

And empower my tongue so that I may illumine
The generations who are still to come
With a spark at least of Your pure serene,

Because by returning to my memory some-
What and being celebrated in these tercets,
Your overallness will be more brought home.

CHAPTER FIFTEEN

A Communion of Sinners ...

> We shall not cease from exploration
> And the end of all our exploring
> Will be to arrive where we started
> And know the place for the first time.
> *T. S. Eliot,* 'Little Gidding'

If you come from a tiny bog village in East Mayo you are, with ninety percent of your school-mates and peers, almost compelled to leave it and to explore the larger and more exciting (?) world beyond. And if you are born into the Catholic Church, its apparently endless inner exploration can sometimes lead you to the beyond of religions and rituals, beliefs and unbeliefs, never dreamt of in the cradle country of your baptism. As a student, priest and academic who has had the opportunity to work, wonder and wander around the world without completely cutting the umbilical chord with village and church of birth and baptism, I have more than once arrived back where I started and got once again to know the place for the first time. So what being a Catholic means to me has a history of exploration and return, adventure and frustration, which forms a much longer story than I can attempt to tell here. What I can attempt to tell, or better to illustrate, is something of the prevailing winds and of the choppy, at times raging, waters which accompanied these voyages around my Father (God) and of the guiding stars and human navigators who got me from time to time safely into the home port, and of what I found and find there.

It is unfortunate, perhaps on reflection providential, that I begin this essay on 'What being a Catholic means to me' on 21 May 2009 bombarded by media accounts of and comments on the 'Report of the Commission to Inquire into Child Abuse' presided over by Judge Sean Ryan which was issued yesterday. I say providential because long overdue, full public rehearsal of their pain for the abused persons, and of the utterly shameful behaviour by some members of the Catholic Church and its leaders, was still essential. It shatters once again the complacency into which believers, clerical and lay, too readily fall when the latest scandal has disappeared from the news headlines. For if my voyages in Catholicism have taught me anything over my sixty years of adulthood, it is that we are first and foremost a communion of sinners who in our best moments aspire to be a communion of saints. Of course there are real and persistent saints among us, mainly invisible and unknown, but we would be well advised, especially if bishops, clergy or religious, to recognise our properly sinful status and the humility, indeed humiliation, that should go with it. How this also allows us to speak of the church as the Body or Bride of Christ, or to share what we call Holy Communion, will re-appear later.

Recognising the sinfulness within and without us, in person and community, is part of the gift of being Catholic. Jesus reserved his harshest words for the self-righteous, the blind leading the blind, the hard of heart, those seeking the first places in synagogue and at table. Some of his unlikely heroes, then as now, were the socially and religiously excluded, the publican at the back of the temple, the Roman soldier who deemed himself unworthy to receive Jesus into his house, the Good Samaritan, and Christ's own criminal companion on the near-by Cross. The list goes on and on. And it is home to that forgiven and forgiving company to which every generation of Catholics must find its way and know the place perhaps for the first time. That is what makes the occasion of this reflection on being a Catholic in the midst of the church in public disgrace truly providential.

Prodigal sons and daughters, as we all always to some extent are, and not necessarily acceptable to the righteous elder brothers and sisters who await us, we are driven by a deeper sense of shame and suffering and then by a hope of welcome and forgiveness that will transform us anew. The prodigally loving Father knows how to celebrate our return, our many returns, as we continue to stray in search of power, privilege, self-righteousness or simply pleasure. We may not be equal to seven times a day, but the falls and stumbles persist.

The providential emergence into the light of recent and current serious falls is not, of course, the first coming of the light, of the Light of the world in Johannine terms, and so more crucially Light for the church. The crux is, as the gospel notes, whether we are willing to acknowledge the Light and act on it. By mid-June we may not be really able to boast of 'green shoots', as those other troubled institutional leaders in banking, finance and politics assert, yet our own glimmers of light may be perceived. The debates in the media, the more positive responses of religious and political leaders and, above all, the strong public reaction to the March of the Abused on Wednesday 10 June, could lead to serious repentance and restitution. But the many words of apology are no substitution for acts of restitution. And how far will such restitution be left to groups and individuals directly responsible, who were also often themselves exploited, oppressed or at best ignored in their limitations as well as in their failures due to internal church structural injustice?

Yet the light is emerging for those with eyes to see, although it may still reveal just more of our own shabbiness. The shabbiness can and will be shed, not indeed without our co-operation and not by our own power. The immediate bearers of the light are undoubtedly the abused. Keeping our eyes and attention fixed on them will draw us more deeply into the forgiving, liberating and transforming light of the God of Jesus Christ, by whose power everything, as Bernanos noted, becomes grace. It may be a slow transformation for all of us. Our inevitable if diminishing resistance, and the righteous anger by the abused, will not disappear overnight or overyear. Yet the grandeur and grace of God will not be finally stayed: 'Because the Holy Ghost over the bent/ World broods with warm breast and with ah! Bright wings.' Hopkins' concluding words to his poem 'God's Grandeur' remain the key to the recovery from the present crisis of the church in Ireland and elsewhere. It is that Holy Spirit that I trust in to enable me to be a genuine if fragile Catholic today. Of course there is more, much more to be said. Only some of it can be briefly rehearsed here ...

Praise as prayer and self-healing are primary tasks for the mutilated church. Out of that self-reform inspired by the Spirit, and the church- reform demanded by the secular world and no less the work of the Spirit, the church in turn attends to the mutilated world, God's world. The Jewish psalms, the long tradition of Christian prayer originating in the prayer which Jesus taught us, provide the models for our praise and its call for ecclesial, social and cosmic healing. 'Hallowed be thy name: thy Kingdom come' summarise these dimensions of praise and healing. Only in the final coming of the kingdom which the church is called to serve will the praise and healing be complete. As the praise issues into service, the charter of service itself is summarised in the Beatitudes, with their further elaboration in the Sermon on the Mount and the extended gospels. Some of these are particularly apt to the broken structures of the church and of the human community as a whole, and indeed to planet earth in its brokenness and despoliation.

The justice seekers and the peacemakers of the Beatitudes outline basic vocations for all church members. These vocations of justice and peace include the whole range of human relationships and communities and their planetary inheritance. At present the justice and peacemaking apply very urgently to the mutilated and divided Catholic Church and to the wider and afflicted Christian community. What it means to be a Catholic today in a practising sense is to be able to translate the praise and prayer into the promotion of justice within the church itself, as demanded and as long prelude to the achieving of ecclesial reconciliation and peace. The perfunctory greeting of peace at Mass or the declining, and often casual, sacramental practice of reconciliation, are no substitute for the surrender to justice and restitution by individual Catholics, by ecclesial power-figures and their protective structures. To be a Catholic is to begin, at serious personal and status cost, on the long road to justice and so to peace.

There are renewal centres on the way. The Eucharist, so central to Catholic Christianity, has the potential to provide food and shelter, healing companionship to the pilgrims for justice and peace and encourage them on their way. If it is not trivialised in indifferent celebration on the one hand or ideologised in some worn-out form on the other, the Eucharist remains at the heart of Catholic life and transformation. To be a Catholic is to enter a community of repentance and humility and so follow the itinerary of Christ's and of the church's life, death and resurrection. The Body of the Lord as community has broader and more profound implications still.

As indicated earlier, Catholic in origin means universal. In recent times and particularly after Vatican II, but not only then, the universal or rather the universe of salvation has tended to follow the range of the reign of God announced by Jesus and indeed that of Creation. It was after all in and through the Word of God, Jesus the Christ, (John, Paul) that all things were created and it was into the world so loved by God that he sent his Son as Saviour. There are many unresolved issues still to be sorted out theologically in the affirmation of the availability of salvation to all within and without the Catholic/Christian community. For this Catholic, the basic affirmation is the undeniable reality of the love of God and of God as love. In such a vision, all human beings are subject to and transformed by the reign of God. We are all daughters and sons of the one God even if that is explicitly recognised by only a few. Whereas as members of one another in Christian terms, where if one suffers we all suffer, in secular terms it is frequently and equivalently asserted that if the human rights of one are violated then the human rights of all are violated. These Christian and secular claims are as equivalent in principle and as they are frequently neglected in practice.

A number of former and perhaps current Irish Catholics have been known to say that they do not believe in an afterlife. Without quibbling about the appropriateness of the phrase 'after-life', I would prefer to reflect on how our earthly bonding as believers or unbelievers may continue beyond the worldly separation of death. Of course the resurrection of Jesus (no simple 'after-life') is the immediate source of our Christian and Catholic belief. Various rationalist attempts to undermine the evidence for it strike me, after years of reflection and occasional hesitations, as invalid. There are older if less powerful supporting arguments and convictions confirming that death is not the end of all. Perhaps for many even committed Catholics the simple absence of the other and the sheer lack of communication is the hardest to bear and the easiest route to loss of faith in the continued existence of the deceased. However, the Catholic understanding of membership of Christ's Body, in principle available to all, enables one to see the departed loved one as still living in Christ and still living if inarticulately in us. The sweep of the reign of God includes naturally those who have gone before us as it will include those who come after us. For that reign establishes a democracy of the living and the dead, whose earthly lives entitled them to that participation. Our memories, their genetic legacies, family and social traditions, and in some cases at least their saintly example, artistic and political achievements, enable our ancestors to continue to influence the development of that great democracy of God's reign or kingdom towards final fulfilment in equality, justice and the peace (*shalom*) that is the flourishing of all creatures together with their God.

That final return to the earth from which we came will indeed be the end of all our exploring and ensure knowing the place for the first and most glorious time, in the company of its Creator God and all our fellow-travellers.

CHAPTER SIXTEEN

… should vatican two survive …

Remembering Austin Flannery OP

The absence of capital and punctuation marks in the title of this chapter is intended to convey the double entendre of the title from the simple question as to whether Vatican II deserves to survive to the conditional, if Vatican II should survive … Perhaps along this line of thought a more disturbing question might be: will Vatican II survive in the spirit of some of its more significant 'letters'? And all this prompted by the recent death of Austin Flannery OP and his tremendous contribution to the continuing life and fruitfulness of the council, not only in Ireland. His documentation, translation and publication of the *Acta* of the council and the follow-up documents, together with his editing of *Doctrine and Life* plus the foundation and publication of further journals and books through Dominican publications, bear witness to a full endorsement and promotion of the work of the council. That takes little account of his wide pastoral and social engagements in liturgy and the arts, in ecumenism, in justice-seeking and peacemaking throughout the island of Ireland. All of which has been recounted more fully elsewhere and should be testimony enough to the success of the council, at least in Ireland. Yet serious doubts remain not about the value of Austin's efforts but about how far the work of council and of its whole-hearted supporters has progressed in the last half-century and that if the present 'snail's pace' continues that work may not prove to be, in the Irish idiom, *obair in aisce*. It may be, although we lack the evidence, that Austin had some such doubts also before his winter light became winter darkness. If these doubts prove to be finally unfounded, as well they may, the Trojan work of Austin will have received its proper recognition.

The questions persist. Why would a theological supporter of the council over the decades now have serious doubts about its vitality/viability? Why would anybody who takes the virtue of Christian hope seriously really doubt that the work of the Holy Spirit at Vatican II would disappear into the sands? What has happened between December 1965 (close of the council) and December 2008 (beginning of this article) to suggest that this council has failed? And who is to blame?

It might be as well to respond to a couple of these questions at once. This is not an attempt to lay blame. It would be unworthy to start from there and impossible to conclude. Secondly, the article is not born of lack of Christian hope so far as the author can tell. Christian hope is not to be, as it frequently is, confused with optimism. And it is not primarily about the church, as a sensitive reading of the gospels and church history might attest. Hope is about the coming kingdom of God, never to be completed in that history and frequently obscured in it. While the church as people of God, in the phrase canonised at Vatican II, remains the great instrument of the Spirit of God in the emergence of the kingdom, it is an ambiguous instrument, obscuring and obstructing the kingdom as well as promoting it. Church history readily confirms this. So our hope for the kingdom does not prevent us from some pessimism about the immediate or medium term future of the church. In this a too positive reading of the 'Signs of the Times', even by the Fathers of Vatican II, may have misled them and us. As no doubt in a purely secular context the expectations raised in the USA and in the wider world by the election of Barack Obama as President of the United States of America may well prove excessive and perish on the stony ground of 'real politik'.

Lest such a parallel between the Spirit-led council and such a secular event seem improper, even blasphemous, it should be remembered that the council itself identified many of the signs of the times with contemporary secular realities, from human rights to third world development to the prospects for justice and peace generally. In one significant and enduring way both the council and the Obama election, as outstanding signs of their times, were symbolic of a new and different world. That the council should have happened to a church now primarily defined as a people and that a black man should be elected President of the USA could prove of more lasting significance that anything else either might achieve. The symbolism, in the deepest even sacramental or Spirit-filled sense, of these two events can never be undone. Whatever practice of un-evangelical power persists in the church, whatever practice of racism persists in the US, the ineradicable symbolic power of these events will continue to subvert such practices. In similar fashion the council Fathers understood truly, that is symbolically, some of the signs of their times. In those restricted terms, the council was successful and will, we trust, always be seen as such.

At one level, Austin Flannery cherished all the documents of Vatican II equally, as evident in the care and attention he exercised to ensure their accurate and readable translation. Inevitably as the council itself made clear even by its designations of constitution, pastoral constitution, decree and declaration, some documents were classified as more significant than others, although not in any mechanical or simply measurable way. The *Declaration on Religious Liberty* for example, both in the intensity of its debates and the consequences of its acceptance, is more significant than the Decree on 'Communications', despite its apparently inferior categorisation. How far Austin Flannery played favourites among the documents at a pastoral or practical level is more difficult to determine, as there is no explicit evidence. However, it is possible to make some educated guesses on the basis of his own pastoral priorities. Such guessing may be more influenced by the concerns of the 'guesser' that by those of Austin. More important may be how far any such preferences illustrate the successes and failures of the council itself.

A crude outline of the concerns of the Council and its subsequent successes and failures might look like this.

The Church: Mystery of God present in the People; Priority of God in People and its developments at parish, diocesan, national and global level.

Failures in development: Sense of mystery still paralysed by bureaucratic structure with its top-down delivery. Fewer especially pastoral priests, fewer engaged lay-people, more bishops, curial officials, administrators.

Liturgy: Mystery of God present in Word, Sacrament and
Worshipping Community.
Increased accessibility and participation but failure to reveal more of the Mystery due to banality of language;
poverty of performance; discriminations and exclusions of
so many believers.
World: Mystery of God present in creation and the human
community; Personal relations in marriage, family and
community; politics of freedom, justice and peace; beauty
in the arts and the environment but not that effective in
either church commitment to artistic work or to protection
of the environment.

A common chant of the critics of Vatican II is that it took away
the 'mystery'. This criticism they apply to the church despite the
first chapter of the *Constitution on the Church* being entitled 'The
Mystery of the Church'. What the critics fail to recognise is that the
council was attempting to clear away the pseudo-mystery con-
cealed in a hierarchy of power rather than of service or in a language and ritual that excluded ninety-nine percent of the church's
members. However, where the council's architects and developers
failed was in not letting the true mystery, the divine mystery,
more fully emerge in church and liturgy as in many other areas.
What Rosemary Haughton decades ago called 'this superbly destructive council' failed in its turn to become 'superbly construc-
tive'. Indeed in recent decades, attempts at destructive cleansing
have been replaced by restorationist attempts at re-covering and
re-concealing in traditionalist clothing the partly exposed true
mystery.

The very different failures by supporters and opponents of the
council are not simply personal to them. Some seeds of failure
were already sown by the council Fathers themselves in their unduly optimistic or pessimistic reading of the times. Other seeds
were rooted in the superficial soil of some enthusiastic supporters
or in the unyielding ground of die-hard opponents. And the blame
then, as now, could be spread further and deeper. In the intervening decades, much has changed and is continuing to change in the
worldly context in which the church must always seek to preach

and promote the kingdom or reign of God. And these changes are assessed very differently within and without the church. In the Western World, from which the Catholic Church is largely dominated despite the radical decline there in church membership and practice, the collapse of the Soviet Empire, the rise of the Muslim community and the sudden collapse of its economic system and dominance offer a whole new set of 'signs of the times', still in need of careful interpretation. The soundings by church leaders are not as yet encouraging. And the precedents of interpreting and responding to earlier and, it would appear, much less threatening developments within and without the church give no great reason for immediate hope. That theologians such as Hans Küng, Edward Schillebeeckx, Charles Curran and Roger Haight, to take some of the more obvious Western examples, should have been censured by the Vatican in the aftermath of the council are witness enough to the decline of that event's liberating influence. More serious, because more rooted in the Church as people, have been the reactions to various versions of the theology of liberation which first emerged with episcopal and even papal blessing in Latin America. The 'preferential option for the poor', the slogan of the movement may still be chanted at the highest level but too many of the deeply engaged people, including theologians such as Gustavo Guttierrez and Jon Sobrino have suffered unnecessary harassment and obstruction from some bishops and the Vatican.

Many other examples might be cited. None of those theologians and church activists could be considered absolutely correct in trying to read the new signs of the times for that is what they were attempting. Yet the Spirit of Vatican II should have allowed them the freedom to make their mistakes as they sought to develop the church's mission anew. Nay-sayers to established conciliar positions, also generally in good faith, were also censured but comparatively few. Their nay-saying was often effective in slowing down much needed clarification and development in areas such as ecumenism, inter-religious dialogue, marital and sexual morality, as well as issues of peace and war. Of course, in speaking of slowing development, this implies some real development during and after the council in the very issues listed. Vatican II has

had its triumphs which have endured even if they have not flour-
ished as they might. For example, the remarkable breakthrough
in inter-church relations then and in the subsequent decade has
remained static for some time. Much the same assessment might
be made of the further realisation of the church as primarily a people and only secondly or thirdly a power-structure. Like Mao's
famous remark on the French Revolution, it may still be too soon
pass judgement on the success or failure of Vatican II even if one
were sure what counted as success or failure in the context.

As symbol at least, the council still lives for many believers.
And that symbol is still a signal of the kingdom of God struggling
to be born for the salvation and final flourishing of the whole of
humanity. It is the Spirit of God and of Jesus Christ which sustains
the life of the symbol. Its historical effects depend after that on the
believing people in whom the divine Mystery is now incarnate.
Should the council survive, the symbol and Spirit will continue
working through that people and all their human allies in search
of the New Creation and New Humanity as St Paul described
them.

Conclusion

The parable of the man going out to sow the seed, with or without
its elaborate Matthean explanation (Mt 13:1-23) is applicable to
Vatican II and its aftermath as it is to so many other gospel enter-
prises. The resistant and distorting ground of rocks and weeds,
the unrelenting opponents and the uncritical enthusiasts, prevented full flourishing. The post-conciliar landscape, littered as it
is with so many dead and infertile spots, retains its quota of living
plants and fertile ground. Only the Spirit knows exactly where
they are and how they might be developed. Listening to and following the Spirit is the prerogative and responsibility of every
church member. Listening lovingly and practically to the Spirit of
God in one another is the continuing lesson of Vatican II and our
only hope of its surviving, as it should. It is a lesson Austin
Flannery had clearly learned, followed and in his practical manner taught.

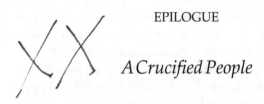

EPILOGUE

A Crucified People

And when the sixth hour had come, there was darkness over the whole earth until the ninth hour. *(Mk 15:33)*

The page-proofs for the book *Theology in Winter Light* were already on my desk when the Report of the Commission of Investigation, Dublin Archdiocese was launched (Thursday 26 November 2009). It would be too much to say that *Theology's Winter Light* was suddenly and completely extinguished. Yes, it was a very dark day for believer and theologian, and impossible to predict when, if ever in this theologian's life, the darkness will ease. However, it did not seem appropriate to let a book with such a title appear so soon after the Report without some reaction, inevitably inadequate, to the new winter darkness. Hence this rather rushed epilogue.

This darkness did not come suddenly. We had been frequently warned of how shocking the report would be. And the Report's predecessors, the Ryan and Ferns Reports might have rendered the caring reader shock proof. Yet as church leaders and faithful members, as well as church critics admitted, the shock was fresh, deep and near paralysing. How long the sense of horror will prevail is hard to know in these catastrophe-ridden headline times.

This brief meditation is an attempt to surrender to the horror as it enveloped the victims of clerical and religious sex-abuse. To be inhabited by the abused in their suffering as a gesture of solidarity and reparation could be a possible basis for our forgiveness and reconciliation; responses from the victims and from their God and ours, to which of course we have no right. The 'we' in question includes not just the individual abusers and their culpably protecting superiors such as bishops but the whole community, certainly of ordained and of professed clerical and religious. That 'we', without all necessarily turning a blind eye, were involved in benefitting from and supporting a culture of institutional prestige and privilege which enabled their abusing colleagues to continue their abuse, immune from the rigours of canon or civil law. This is not in any way to diminish the moral responsibility of the active abusers and their need to be brought to justice. It maybe what Marie Keenan was suggesting on the *Prime Time* programme on Thursday of the launch, that failing to recognise and radically re-form that wider cultural context in the church could frustrate the most effective child protection measures in the future, and allow for a recurrence of the same or similar problems.

Public reaction to the Reports expressed, first of all, justified outrage at the crimes of abuse inflicted on children, secondly in-dignation at the negligence of church authorities in permitting these to continue and, thirdly sharp criticism of the persistent neglect by the civil authorities of their duties in intervening to pre-vent further crimes and to investigate and prosecute those priests and religious accused. This last was particularly evident in the aftermath of the Murphy report. All of these demand fuller exam-ination and follow-up if there is to be any hope of restorative just-ice for the past and adequate protection in the future.

Although we have been here before, vocal responses from both church and civil leaders to date may sound a more authentic note just now. This is particularly true of the man in the eye of the storm, Archbishop Diarmuid Martin. Yet fine words, however sincere, do not readily transform into action, especially the radi-cally reforming action that seems called for.

Some fifteen years ago as these problems were breaking sur-face here and elsewhere, Bishop Michael Murphy of Cork called for a National Assembly (or Synod), representative of all strands of Irish Catholic life, bishops, priests, religious and laypeople to address the challenges to faith and church that he and many others saw developing in the years ahead. It never happened of course, and there seems little appetite for it even now that these problems have flooded in. The episcopal church may not have been fully prepared for it then, although preparations could have been begun. That same body may be even more resistant to it now. Yet the presence and power and indeed grace of the now openly 'crucified people', of the clerically and religiously abused, may provide the basis, the energy and the direction for the healing and transformation which the whole church so badly needs.

A Crucified People

Archbishop Oscar Romero may have been the first person to invoke the phrase 'a crucified people' to describe the poor and oppressed of El Salvador. Such remarks and his commitment to these people eventually cost him his life. It was the supporting theologians, Ignacio Ellacuria, also martyred in El Salvador, and Jon Sobrino who gave the phrase theological substance. Any serious meditation on the recent reports, Ryan and Murphy, would find the Romero phrase especially apt in describing the abused and, in the case of Murphy if to a lesser extent, in describing their families. An even deeper dimension of the isolation, loneliness and pain of crucifixion emerges in Ryan where the institutionalised children are deprived of family, sometimes of name and of personal identity and of any prospect of work or career. The abuse recorded in both Reports provides the starting point for the further course of this meditation.

Living with the Crucified People

The accounts of the passion and death of Jesus Christ in the gospels are at the heart of our Christian discipleship, its practice and spirituality. The Stations of the Cross, The Sorrowful Mysteries of the Rosary, the Good Friday Ceremonies and, of course, the daily and weekly Eucharist confront us in various symbolic and sacramental ways with the direction and depth of the Christian journey. At critical moments in our lives and in those in our care we seek consolation and help in meditating on and absorbing the sufferings of Christ. They embody, as key-interpretation, the vulnerability, finitude and mortality of ourselves and others. For theologians such as Sobrino and many more third-world disciples, the sufferings of the oppressed poor and excluded provide a here and now representation, indeed the re-enactment of the prosecution, torture and death of Jesus Christ. 'As long as you did it to one of these least ones you did it to me' (Mt

25:40). In working with people in Africa and Asia whose poverty
and oppression was compounded by hunger and disease, HIV
and Aids, I felt the force of Romero's original remark. It seems no
less forceful in facing up to the phenomenon of sexually abused
children.

The 'passion' accounts of the sufferings of the abused in the
Ryan and Murphy Reports should be central to the Catholic
Church, particularly its leaders as bishops, priests and religious,
as it attempts to respond. Of course, many bishops, priests and
others have given at least a cursory reading to the full reports as
circulated to them or as presented on the Internet. Much more is
called for if they are to be inhabited to the point of really painful
solidarity with the abused. Sections of the reports focusing on the
detail of the suffering should form part of their daily prayerful
meditation in conjunction with parallel gospel readings from
Christ's passion narrative. By this practice their protective ar-
mour may be breached and they will get beyond the recent, careful and no doubt sincere apologies and the promises of better and
better implemented guidelines. Only by the repeated surrender
to the recorded sufferings of those for whom they had responsibility will they undergo the grace of humiliation without which
any claim to humility remains unreal. In this context, salvation for
church personnel, community and institution may emerge from
the marginalised by the saving grace of God.

This practice is not simply for individuals at whatever level of
church. Church is and foremost community, the People of God
and the Body of Christ. So the abused and the abusers and their
protectors and indeed the whole community of believers is involved in its current shameful suffering. In seeking to overcome
the shame and heal the suffering of the Body of Christ solidarity
with one another and with Christ on the cross must be developed
by communal services or practices in churches, community centres,
homes or wherever. These services might have an introductory
greeting and kiss of peace, followed by readings from the Reports
on particular abuse cases both physical and sexual and then a
silent meditative prayer. After that, a suitable gospel passage on
Christ's passion and death, then a further silent prayer might be

followed by a shared vocal reflection by all present who are willing to participate. A suitable hymn or psalm might lead into a brief penitential rite and conclude with mutual acceptance, if the time is not yet ripe for reconciliation in fuller sense, as it probably will not be on the first occasion. Too much is too often crammed into our liturgical services, including the Eucharist. We might be content on the first occasion with just greetings, prayers, vocal and silent, a selection of readings as listed, a brief and shared commentary and a warm, personal and communal farewell with the commitment to meet again soon. Suggestions for suitable readings are appended at the end of this chapter.

The service might be organised on a parish level with local priests and faithful, and if possible some abused and abusers. This, however, may be difficult but should be pursued later if necessary. The local bishop should be invited, but as a simple member of community. A small committee might be asked to prepare the service. Priests and religious should not be play prominent roles although they probably will be necessary facilitators.

This brief reflection on the humiliation and conversion into healing and salvation for church leaders and other members, through solidarity in suffering of a profound kind with the abused, and the attempt to sketch a liturgy to embody all that, are no more than an early reaction. Many other and perhaps better proposals may well emerge. In any event, the prosecution of offenders of abuse and its cover-up must be followed up, codes for the future protection of children must be strengthened and rigorously implemented. In that context, bishops and superiors who have been found seriously negligent as supervisors (*epi-scopi*) of abusers should resign. This should be a matter of honour for them as they seek to respond to the abused and to serve the wider church in new ways, perhaps by working with other deprived groups in the country or returning to a more intellectual career or just as curates so badly needed in so many places. This presumes that there are no criminal charges to be answered.

Essential as all the measures listed above are, of themselves they will not overcome the real and recurring deeper crisis in the church. That crisis calls for truly radical change in culture and structures which are intimately connected in forming the present institutional church. One obvious weakness in the current system is the manner of appointment of bishops with its criteria of a very narrow orthodoxy and the power of appointment confined to the Vatican, with very little attention to local voices and resources. That again is a symptom of a deeper cultural malaise where laity remain basically untrustworthy and so powerless, while clergy remain exclusively male and celibate and largely powerless in policy-making terms. The practice of bishops meeting alone and deciding church policy and practice has again and again proved its inadequacy. One could go on listing such characteristics of the failed culture and structures of the present Irish church. Only local and national assemblies with the insights of some independent think-tanks could begin to address the immense theological, pastoral and spiritual challenges that may yet overwhelm the whole Irish church.

Service texts

Any one of the four gospel passion narratives would provide plenty of material. As an example, I choose Matthew and list it under a number of headings which might be suitable for a particular service. However, as these texts overlap with one another and with the other gospels, a quite different more continuous approach to sections of the passion accounts might be chosen. At the beginning or end of each service the description in Matthew 25: 31-40 might be read. By persons and themes the following readings might be selected for various occasions, assuming there will be more than one such service.

The Gospel of Matthew:
Judas: Matthew 26:14-16, 20-25, 47-50; Mt: 27:3-10.
Peter: Mt 26:30-35, 40, 57-77
Disciples: Mt 26:36-43, 55-56

Sufferings of Jesus.
Agony in the Garden: Mt 26:36-46
Before Caiaphas: Mt 26:57-68
Before Pilate: Mt 27:11-26
Abuse and Crucifixion: Mt 27:27-50

The Murphy and Ryan Reports

These Reports are very extensive in terms of the abused, the abusers, the abuse and the failure of the 'supervisors', so something from each might be included in each service. However, it might be useful to concentrate on particular sections of the Reports.

For Murphy I suggest Part 2, Chapters 12, 13, 24 and 29. As these are all long, one must again select not only between but within the chapters. They do, however, give a very good flavour of what happened and how we failed.

For the Ryan Report I suggest Chapters 7 and 9 from Volume III as they record both male and female abuse in institutions. A drastic selection will need to be made while retaining the horrors recorded.

All these texts can be accessed on various sites on the Internet. The printed texts are available from the Government Publications Office, Molesworth St, Dublin at a reasonable price.

Enda McDonagh, Maynooth
3 December 2009